GETTING THE MONEY YOU NEED:

Practical Solutions for
Financing Your Small Business

GETTING THE MONEY YOU NEED:
Practical Solutions for Financing Your Small Business

Gibson Heath

IRWIN
Professional Publishing

Chicago • Bogatá • Boston • Buenos Aires • Caracas
London • Madrid • Mexico City • Sydney • Toronto

This book is dedicated to the people of Antonito, Colorado. Thank you for putting up with me during its writing.

Particular thanks to the founders and members of Arco Iris Center for Community Development—Richard, Sr. Kay, Demetrio and Olive, Moses, Virginia S. and Michael, Little Felix, Andrew G. Lawrence, Robert, and Ruvel. Thanks also to my friends and acquaintances—Ida, Joven, Burt, Gary, Andrew P., Cletus, Virginia J., Bertha, Ramona, Frederick; and to my good neighbors—Margarita, Estella, Rosa, Carmen, Maria, Juanita, and Juaquin.

Always remember how fortunate you are to live in a place where angels kiss the earth.

Senior sponsoring editor:	Amy Hollands Gaber
Project editor:	Paula M. Buschman
Production supervisor:	Jon Christopher
Designer:	Laurie J. Entringer
Compositor:	Douglas & Gayle, Ltd.
Typeface:	11/13 Palatino
Printer:	Buxton & Skinner

Library of Congress Cataloging-in-Publication Data

Heath, Gibson.
  Getting the money you need : practical solutions for financing your small business / Gibson Heath.
    p. cm.
  Includes index.
  ISBN 1-55623-935-1
  1. Small business—Finance. I. Title.
HG4027.7.H422 1995
658.15'224—dc20   95-2027
                                               CIP

Printed in the United States of America

1 2 3 4 5 6 7 8 9 0 BS 2 1 0 9 8 7 6 5

Introduction

Take heart: you're not alone in your search for small business funding. There are people willing and able to help.

Sometimes it's a simple matter of organizing your paperwork in an acceptable manner. In other cases, it may involve your learning and pursuing new borrowing applications.

This book will give you practical suggestions for achieving your financing goals regardless of the individual challenges you face. Remember the adage, "Where there is a will, there is a way." Your determination is key to your success.

Small business owners are take-charge individualists. The inherent knowledge that you can make things happen is a powerful entrepreneurial financing tool. Historically, that can-do attitude is a pervasive theme in our collective national mentality.

We are a country of problem solvers. Current small business funding strategies are prime examples. In many geographical areas, it has become so difficult to get traditional small loans that people ban together in grassroots organizations to borrow and lend money.

These new pioneers are leading the way. Fresh trends in small business financing are on the horizon, and you can take part and benefit.

In many instances, it's not a case of reinventing the wheel. Instead, it's a process of thinking through old concepts and using workable pieces. New approaches such as microenterprise lending are not as complicated as the name might sound. Instead, they offer simple solutions founded on old fashioned trust principles. Basically, they reach back to earlier years when individuals gave their word as collateral for loan repayment. Personal integrity and a desire for respect within the community provide the loan guarantees.

Today, there is a healthy resurgence of community involvement and personal responsibility. In financing there is a trend toward reevaluation of present standards. From inner city neighborhoods to rural chambers of commerce, there is a new desire to seek out small business funding programs that are more appropriate to community needs.

You can participate and help change things for the better. Reach out, extend and take a helping hand. At the very core, new small business funding practices are as much about self-reliance and community caring as they are about economics.

Grassroots demand and supply principles are testing corporate policy. If it's economically unfeasible for banks to make small loans, perhaps it's time for communities to take action.

Keep in mind, however, that the new funding revolution is characterized by its subtlety. Success and power come from a quiet practicality: Put simply, target the problem and find a community-based way to resolve it. Don't challenge traditional lending sources; find a way to make them part of the solution.

As a nation, we've weathered some bad times; now, let's share prosperity, and let's do it with confidence. Remember, the marketplace is a great equalizer. The more loan pools we create and the more self-sufficient we become, the more likely it will be that banks, government, foundations, and big businesses will want to get involved. Don't ask for an umbrella. Do a rain dance, *create the rain!*

Small businesses are the fastest growing segment of the U.S. economy. They provide *all* new jobs. They create wealth. As small business owners, *you are the future.*

As a nation, we're counting on you. What's more, we know you can succeed. When things get tough, remember that wonderful rock and roll lyric, "You can't always get what you want; but if you try sometime, you just might find, you get what you need."[1]

We're all here to help. When you need a hand, just ask. Best of luck. Go get 'em.

Gibson Heath
Denver, Colorado

---

[1]Rolling Stones, Mick Jagger/Keith Richards, *Satisfaction*, 1967.

ACKNOWLEDGEMENTS

No book is the sole product of the writer's endeavors. The author conceives the idea, but others, acting as sounding boards, friends, advisors, researchers, and publishers, give it texture, dimension, and form. This book would not be possible if not for the help and kindness of many individuals.

I owe a special word of thanks to my agent, Peter Miller, and my publisher, Irwin Professional Publishers, and Ralph Rieves, for adjusting to my timetable. Though the circumstances were extraordinary, your patience was greatly appreciated.

Many thanks to Sondra Maher for her hours of research, checking and rechecking names and addresses. Thanks to Peggy Clark, Tracy Houston, Bob Friedman, CELI founding members, Greg Cooke, Kent Briggs, and David Leavitt for sharing information and guidance. For friendship, love, and appropriate prodding, thanks Nell, Bayne, Laurie, Tim, Julia, Jayne, and Bob.

I also offer my gratitude and undying appreciation to the hard-working, dedicated staff at Irwin Professional Publishing who shaped and promoted the final product: Project Editor, Paula Buschman; Production Supervisor, Jon Christopher; Designer, Laurie Entringer; Executive Editor, Amy Hollands Gaber, and Tiffany Dykes, Marketing Manager.

And most of all to the people who are in the field making microenterprise happen on a daily basis, the founders and members of AEO, and all the new pioneers in community funding.

You are all a blessing and inspiration. Thank you with all my heart.

GH

Contents

Chapter One

A Good Start

Though many roads lead to small business ownership, three entrepreneur motivations are typical: necessity, independence, and lifelong dreams.

Some individuals have responsibilities at home, such as caring for small children or an elderly parent, for example. Needing extra cash, they might start a small home-based business in their spare time.

Other people want independence. Using a telephone, computer, modem, and fax machine, they choose a "lone-eagle" business base in a remote geographical area to suit their lifestyle.

For others, owning their own business is a dream come true. Often, they spend years working for big corporations, but use their leisure time preparing for their future small firm. Some buy franchises, while others stumble upon a great product and envision potential opportunities.

All entrepreneurs want control of their own destiny. They pursue business avenues that offer self-sufficiency.

Starting a business is an exciting but exacting proposition. In the beginning, most entrepreneurs take a great deal of time to think about all the possibilities—good and bad.

Those of you who move forward are comfortable with your evaluations because you believe in your product or service and you have confidence in your ability to perform. You are enthusiastic about the business's future, and you do everything you can to ensure success.

Though you have your own unique small business style, you have a great deal in common with your fellow entrepreneurs, too. You are all independent adventurers. You are intuitive and creative. You assess situations quickly and adapt appropriately. You are a risk-taker.

Unfortunately, some of the very characteristics that make you an accomplished entrepreneur put you at odds with traditional financial thinking. Small business owners and financiers admire one another from a distance, but often don't speak the same language.

TARGET AUDIENCE

The information in this book will help you bridge the gap. Please keep in mind that no single resource is all-inclusive. While this book contains financial references pertaining to all small businesses, it specifically targets firms one to three years old with fewer than 10 employees.

For larger companies and veteran small business owners, this manual will offer a solid review of traditional resources as well as an update on new alternatives. Start-up firms can use the information herein to plan a course of action.

OVERVIEW

This book contains eight chapters. Whether you need to read it from cover to cover depends on your level of financial expertise and funding needs. However, a quick read of certain chapters will answer many important questions about financing techniques and recent changes in lending practices. Specifically recommended passages include: "A Good Start," "Financing through Banks," "Alternative Nonbank Financing Options," and "Microenterprise Lending Programs." If you are in a community that has relatively few entrepreneur financing options, Chapter Eight, "Developing Community Loan Funds," is a significant read, too.

In addition to text information, there are three resource chapters: "Federal Government Sources," "State Programs," and "Index: Microenterprise Loan Programs." Each chapter describes the plan. Specific projects also illustrate lending amounts, who qualifies, required paperwork, and realistic time frames. Resource names, addresses, and phone numbers are listed for your convenience.

FUNDING

Most start-up small businesses are self-funded. Typically, new companies work on a pay-as-you-go basis to augment financing. This operating style requires that customers pay COD for products and make regular installments for services. In turn, the new business generally reimburses its suppliers on COD terms, too.

As these firms grow in the early months, income from sales helps them boot-strap up one notch at a time. While this rapid dollar turnover creates quick cash flow, it's not necessarily efficient nor is it accepted as a professional business practice. At some point in the first 18 to 36 months, growing companies need additional money for product development, inventory, operating expenses, marketing, as well as for establishing and extending credit terms.

Many entrepreneurs feel uncomfortable when seeking outside financing. However, if you view your situation as a positive growth step, fund-raising will be less daunting. Some of the characteristics that helped you launch your business—enthusiasm, dedication, salesmanship—will help you when you present your funding proposal.

Remember, too, that money is a product. It's available to you either as a loan or as an investment. Banks, lenders, and investors want your business. They market capital through various financing plans, much as you market your product.

Banks.   While commercial lending is highly regulated and many rules apply, the goal is making loans. Borrowing money is easier if you understand the loan process. Although no one can guarantee that your firm gets a small business loan, you can improve the odds in your favor by knowing the correct steps and establishing timely, realistic goals. Chapter Two, "Financing through Banks" provides basic information on commercial lending.

Other Options.   Not all funding solutions are obvious. There are also indirect ways to improve your financial situation.

In any small firm, changes take place rapidly. To minimize expenses and maximize cash, you should evaluate the way you do business on a regular basis.

When you need new office equipment, for example, consider the advantages and disadvantages of lease financing. Bartering your goods or services for items you need is another option. Renting versus owning your office location is also a consideration.

In short, it's important to keep in mind that every business decision you make directly affects your cash flow. Chapter Three, "Alternative Nonbank Financing Options," reviews ways you can preserve your cash by making wise choices one day at a time.

The aforementioned funding solutions are all resources that allow you to maintain private ownership. As such, they do not require selling stock in your company. As an informed consumer, you should also know about investor financing options available to you.

Venture capital.   It is also possible that your business is a prime candidate for outside investment. Investors have their own criteria when evaluating business opportunities. It's important to know what they look for and whether your company fits that pattern.

A basic understanding of investment capital pros and cons is valuable to all small businesses. It may open doors to new opportunities. It may convince you that equity financing is not for you. Either way, knowledge of how it works gives you decision-making tools. Chapter Four, "Investment in Your Business: Venture Capital, Initial Public Offerings, and Other Options," gives fundamental data on equity participation in small business ventures.

Federal government sources.   In the past, a few negative connotations were associated with government loan projects. Most complaints stemmed from excess paperwork and time frames. However, today, many state and federal programs serve as models for future private lending plans.

For example, the Small Business Administration (SBA) has several lending programs worthy of your consideration. While a few make loans directly to you, most SBA plans are loan guarantees. Those programs require a minimum of paperwork and take less than two weeks to set in motion. If your loan is refused, the SBA will tell you why and also give you ideas on improving your loan package. The agency will offer suggestions for other local resources, too.

Chapter Five, "Federal Government Sources," looks at available direct and indirect funding programs. A listing of various types of government assistance is in this section, followed by a resource segment.

State programs. Most state-sponsored small business programs are worthy of your consideration. Some provide training only. These projects help you prepare a business plan and loan package. Other state programs offer direct and indirect loans.

Many state programs are innovative and exciting. Participation in them gives the small business owner a definitive edge. A complete listing of state-sponsored small business plans is found in Chapter Six—"State Programs."

Microenterprise lending. Microenterprise lending is a new trend in U.S. small business funding that deserves your investigation. Three key points about microlending are noteworthy:

- Loan amounts. As the name implies, a microloan is a very small loan made to an entrepreneur. However, you should know that since this is a new discipline, per-request loan maximums vary tremendously. While some loan pools extend individual loans up to only $1,000, others range upward to $25,000.
- Collateral. Characteristically, microloan pools require less collateral than other lending funds. Of course, this differs with each program, but, on the whole, criteria are relaxed.
- Technical assistance. A key factor of microenterprise loans is the emphasis on technical assistance. Some programs provide training directly as part of the lending package. Others allow a budget for private consultants within the loan.

Microenterprise loan funds began as a grassroots solution to small business funding in the early 90s. Most programs are adaptations of successful Third World entrepreneurial financing plans. As the field develops in the United States, learn-as-you-go changes are implemented and shared between funds.

While some problems are inevitable in any new discipline, on the whole, microlending projects offer significant lending alternatives. What's more, the new movement is encouraging government and commercial lenders to rethink their small business lending approach.

Chapter Seven, "Microenterprise Lending Programs," gives a brief history, provides definitions, and indexes many microloan funds.

Community loan funds.   Fortunately, some U.S. locations offer entrepreneurs a wide variety of financial options. However, if you are in a geographical area that has limited access to capital, you should learn about fund development. Building a community lending pool takes time, effort, and team work, but the end results merit your commitment.

Help is available. Entrepreneurial financing is becoming big business. Government and commercial sources are interested in new ideas.

Nonprofit microlending groups are pioneering the field. They have guidelines, supportive data, and plentiful advice.

Though money is tight, outside capital is a possibility. Some sources offer cash, while others guarantee against a certain percentage of funds raised or dollars loaned.

Community involvement is also key. The prospects are endless because helping small companies grow has a ripple effect. Expanding firms hire workers who, in turn, spend their paychecks at other neighborhood establishments. Everyone benefits from local small business development.

Chapter Eight, "Developing Community Loan Funds," will give you pointers on establishing a loan pool. Outside resources are also listed. These organizations and individuals know the ropes. They can help you avoid pitfalls and design a solid program.

HOME-BASED BUSINESSES

Today, many entrepreneurs choose to work from their homes. In effect, home-based businesses are the economic phenomenon of the 1990s. While tracking this development is difficult because not all home-based businesses are formalized, experts believe the home office segment of the Small Office Home Office (SOHO) industry is rapidly growing. "According to LINK Resources, more than 41 million Americans do some part of their work from their homes. And this growth has increased by more than 50 percent since 1989. More than 12 million of these are full-time home-based businesses."[1]

There are a number of reasons why home-based businesses work well. Equipment that was once cost-prohibitive now is reasonably obtainable. Improvements in telecommunications have paved the way for easier interaction. Advances in computer technology make it practical to perform many business tasks from a nontraditional location. For example, a two-line telephone and a moderately priced personal computer with fax, modem, and laser printer give home-based entrepreneurs a professional business edge.

Stereotypes about working from home are changing as well. As major corporations relax their rules regarding employees working at home, the notion gains wider acceptability.

Modifications in contemporary family life impact this situation, too. Multigenerational and one-parent households, which require more home time, are on the rise.

Working at home has advantages. Flexible hours improve productivity, while casual dress and warm surroundings increase comfort.

However, home-based businesses face some obstacles as well. Zoning laws, for example, may restrict use of house space, signage, parking, and business classification. The Internal Revenue Service (IRS) applies strict criteria for home/office allowances, too, particularly if you also use other outside locations.

Financing is one problem commonly shared by many home-based entrepreneurs, because most home businesses are in the service sector. Consequently, traditional company assets such as real estate, inventory, and equipment usually are not part of a home-based business infrastructure.

Sometimes it's a frustrating situation. However, you should remember that there are some new trends in financing. The home-based business sector is growing quickly. Ultimately, the marketplace responds to "demand and supply" principles. And *money* is a product.

---

[1]Paul and Sarah Edwards, "Working from Home Forum," *Points West Special: Work Shifting,* Center for New West, November 1994.

STRAIGHT CREDIT VERSUS THE PROGRAM APPROACH TO LENDING

Banks are private enterprises and, as such, they are in business to make money. They can accomplish that goal only if it is a sure bet they will get repaid for any loans dispersed.

One reason banks typically want three years' financial statements from a small business before granting a loan is that national statistics indicate 50 percent of all small businesses terminate within the first 4.25 years.[2] Small firms that are doing well in the first three years are likely to succeed well beyond that critical point.

Some individuals in finance and public agencies take the posture that business failures are a natural form of economic attrition. They assume that owners who fail learn from errors made in the first business and apply those lessons to future successful enterprises.

However, findings don't support that theory. Instead, they show that, regardless of firm size, business failures have a negative effect on the economy through lost jobs, unpaid loans, and owner recovery time.

Traditionally, banks advance credit, but maintain a hands-off attitude when it comes to giving customers small business advice. That taboo is born of the notion that any guidance given might potentially alter the business course. In the event the company fails, the bank might sustain some degree of liability for advice offered and forfeit any loan extended.

Many bankers who enjoy working with small firms feel their hands are tied. Too, entrepreneurs regard bankers as professionals and often seek their input.

Fortunately, new nonbank lending programs generally include some degree of technical assistance and training. This business support aspect brings a new, practical dimension to enterprise funding.

There is a downside, however. Overhead costs for these "service provider" agencies giving advice and advancing loans are typically much higher than those sustained by banks. Agencies not only review business loan paperwork, but also provide field agents,

---

[2]United States Small Business Administration, *The State of Small Business: A Report of the President*, 1992.

who assist borrowers in all aspects of small business ownership on a regular basis. That practice requires additional personnel and expense. While these nonprofits charge higher interest rates than banks and often add on fees, there is a disparity spread between income generated and portfolio management cost.

On the other hand, most agencies feel the extra outlay is justifiable. Supplementary benefits get small firms off to a good start and keep them on sound footing throughout difficult growth stages.

Typically, there are five areas in which service-provider agencies help borrowers:

- Education: Technical assistance and training are provided in structured workshops or informally on an as-needed basis.
- Mentoring: Loan recipients are paired with an experienced volunteer counselor.
- Peer groups: Borrowers meet together at regularly scheduled times to discuss their progress, difficulties, and successes.
- Partnering: Small firms are matched with larger companies that may buy their products or services. These corporations also often assist in technical areas such as sophisticated computer access or international trade issues.
- Financing: Service-provider agencies offer flexible loan plans that suit the individual borrower's needs and ability to repay.

Two other advantages of program lending are communication and control. In most instances, service-provider agencies maintain an ongoing dialogue with their clients. Through on-site visits and phone calls, they preserve constant communication that helps identify problems and solutions early on.

Agencies maintain portfolio control through smaller but more frequent loan payment plans. Depending on the loan size, available collateral, and cash flow, clients may make payments as often as once a week. If a payment is late, agency personnel, peer group members, and mentors find out why. Generally, advice and peer pressure get the borrower back on track quickly.

A strict, credit-only approach to lending works well for experienced small businesses. Seasoned entrepreneurs know the ropes.

A program approach to lending fills in the gaps. Service-provider agencies give start-ups and young, struggling businesses more than money. They teach skills, provide resources, offer advice, and bolster confidence. The extra cost for these services is worth the price. It often means the difference between small business failure or success.

DEFINING *SMALL BUSINESS*

Historic definitions contribute to the confusion about what small businesses need. Conventional government notions suggest that a small company is any firm with 100 or fewer employees. That definition is too broad.

In 1991, according to Reid Gearhart, a Dun & Bradstreet analyst, 85 to 90 percent of all businesses in the United States had fewer than 20 employees.[3]

However, specific facts about these businesses are not recorded by any federal agency. The only annotated information available is from Unemployment Insurance (UI), which simply denotes the number of employees.

> According to UI data, there were 5.8 million businesses with employees in 1991, up from 4.7 million in 1981. All but about 7,000 of these are small businesses with fewer than 500 employees.[4]

Evaluating and predicting trends in small business borrowing is difficult without appropriate statistical data. Clear, accurate information is needed to design sound strategies for future funding.

There are some positive steps in the right direction. The U.S. government included 227 additions to the *Standard Industrial Classification Manual* (SIC) in 1992. Small firms dominate *all* those new areas. SIC codes not only show "who does what," but also provide payroll data by business classification.

At the grassroots level, microenterprise lenders are developing their own definitions for tracking small businesses. Accord-

---

[3]Mary Rowland, "Why Small Businesses Are Failing," *The New York Times*, 1991.
[4]Rowland, ibid

ing to the Self-Employment Learning Project (SELP),[5] "the term *self-employment* refers to the working status of a business owner who works for himself or herself for more than 10 hours per week. A self-employed person may own and operate a *microenterprise* of very few employees. Although these two terms are used interchangeably, *self-employment* refers to the working status of the business owner while *microenterprise* refers to a very small business."[6]

Other terms acknowledge business age and growth. For example, *emerging business* denotes a young but strong company adding jobs, usually in excess of five employees. The expression *bankable small business* generally recognizes a firm with at least a three-year track record, dependable cash flow and reasonable access to traditional financing.

New small business definitions simplify statistical analysis. Furthermore, with this data, researchers can help lenders accurately estimate future small firm borrowing and technical assistance needs. And that's a major strategic step forward.

If you are like most small business owners, you are extraordinarily busy. As the adage goes, "there aren't enough hours in a day." However, you should keep in mind that learning financing skills will save time. There are added bonuses, too. Knowledge will give you confidence and help you obtain the money you need to make your business grow.

---

[5]Self-Employment Learning Project (SELP) is a three-year research program undertaken to study microenterprise development programs in the United States. For this study, five projects, representing different philosophies and geographic locations, were selected.

[6]Margaret Clark, "Self-Employment Learning Project," *Assisting the Smallest Businesses*, Aspen Institute, 1993.

Chapter Two

Financing through Banks

Banks play a big role in your small business. Regardless of whether you get the money you want from a commercial lender or another funding source, you need a solid banking relationship.

There are two good reasons why this is true. First, banks have standard loan paperwork requirements that are commonplace throughout all other lending systems. While there are many funding avenues, knowing what documents banks require will help you prepare for all types of financing.

Second, conducting business via bank-to-bank transactions is a universally accepted procedure. A business checking account gives you a convenient way to pay your bills and track customer receipts. Most lenders will expect you to have a professional banking relationship. Some funding sources, such as microenterprise loan programs, will help you establish a banking affiliation if you don't have one.

Basic Requirements for All Funding Methods

While there are many different funding avenues available to you as a small business owner, there are two basic steps you need to take before seeking funds: (1) prepare a business plan and (2) properly organize your financial records.

The plan. Your business plan is the road map that navigates your company. It describes your business concept and how it works, defines your market and competition, explains cash flow peaks and valleys, emphasizes the strengths and capabilities of the management team, and illustrates why your company is a good credit risk.

Writing a business plan helps you focus your business strategy. It's an important tool for you and for your funding source. However, a completed plan does not lock you into a particular course; it is simply a guide. As the company grows, review the plan regularly. Over time, it may need revisions to target new opportunities.

Aspects of the plan vary because all businesses are different. However, there are key sections that are standard in any plan. Following this outline will get you started on the right foot.

• Executive summary. This is the summation of the entire plan. It should be no more than two or three pages. Though it appears first, it is written last. The intention of the summary is to provoke reader interest. It should make the reader want to know more about your business concept.

• Business description. This section gives the history of your business and explains your overall concept. It should explain how the business started, how it evolved, and what it does. If the company is a start-up, describe the business idea and the direction it will take.

• Management and organizational structure. This segment tells who runs the business and how individuals work together. Who are the members of the management team? What is the experience of the key players? What are their accomplishments in their fields of expertise? What are their roles in the business?

How does company management move from one individual to the next? What are the duties of key staff members, and how do they relate to each other? Do certain responsibilities overlap?

A management flowchart might be appropriate in this section to help the reader visualize your company organization.

• Product or service. This portion of the plan describes what you sell. In layman's terms, explain how your product or service developed and why it is unique. Briefly discuss production quality controls. How are raw materials secured? Who are your suppliers? What process is involved in making your product? What are the time tables from inception to product sale? Do you own a patent?

If yours is a service company, define your scope of work. Do you use prepared materials to conduct your business? Did you develop those materials? Are they copyright or trademark protected?

What process is followed from the day you begin working with a client until contract completion? Is there a clear beginning and end to your work? Are there typical time frames?

• Competition and market share. This section provides information on your competitive status. How many other firms provide a product or service that is similar? What are the comparisons? How do their price structures correlate to yours? What is your market share? Do you anticipate an increase in market share? If so, will that come from product improvement, a new product, or increased marketing? Can you garner the lead in your market? How will your product or service continue its success? If the general economy falters, will the demand for your product or service diminish?

• Marketing plan. This segment outlines your marketing strategy and future marketing plans. How do you define your target market? What type of marketing reaches that audience best? What are your current marketing costs? Of your total annual budget, what percentage represents marketing expenses? Do you market directly? Do you use an advertising agency? Do you count on repeat business or customer referrals? How do you follow up on marketing leads? What percentage of product or service inquiries result in completed sales?

• Growth projections. If you executed all the elements of your business plan, what would happen? How much growth would your company realize? If yours is an existing company, how does this growth relate to growth patterns over the last few years? Why might your firm grow notably in the future? Will growth require additional time and dollars for marketing? Are there anticipated research and development expenses? Do you expect necessary new equipment purchases? Will growth mean adding to your existing labor force? How will growth benefits outweigh expansion costs?

• Contingency plan. This section anticipates risks in your plan. What auxiliary actions might you take if unforseen circumstances alter your business success? What happens to cash flow if sales targets aren't obtainable? If a key staff person leaves or is unable to complete his or her responsibilities, what happens? What if labor or goods costs escalate? Are labor problems likely? How do you anticipate dealing with them? What external factors could cause problems with goods shipment and product distribution? If you

are a sole proprietor in a service business, what happens if you get
sick? How will any adversity or miscalculation affect your company? What is your back-up plan to handle those situations, should
they arise?

• Financials. All appropriate financial information should be
in this section. That includes pro forma and cash flow analyses
showing expected figures by month for the first year and quarterly for the next two to three years. Also include complete interim
financials as well as the most recent fiscal year-end financial statement for the business. (See the segment, "Organizing Financial
Records" following.)

• Appendix. The appendix should contain specific information
that is germane to sections of the plan. For example, if the plan is
geared around precise individual expertise, that person's résumé
should appear in the appendix. If the plan relies on the perfection
of a particular product, field-test results should be summarized in
this section. Long-term contracts or extensive lease agreements
that impact the business might also be considered for inclusion.
In addition, any other relevant document should be noted. For example, if your marketing plan is based on outside studies conducted by others, include copies.

A well-constructed business plan is a valuable asset to any business. It helps you stay on target and gives funding sources a good
grasp of your company strategies and projections, as well.

If possible, use computer-generated graphics to illustrate key
points in the plan. Graphics add a professional touch.

Your plan should extend out at least one year. However, funding sources prefer a three- to five-year outlook.

If you are preparing your business plan on your own, there are
many good books on the market to guide you through the process.
Reliable computer programs are also available.

Several agencies offer help in business plan preparation. See
Chapter Five, "Federal Government Sources," for information regarding Small Business Administration-sponsored Small Business
Development Centers (SBDCs). There are over 600 locations throughout the country. Most SBDCs offer classes and one-on-one assistance with business plans, marketing plans, and financials.

If you are self-employed in a start-up business situation or your
borrowing needs are under $25,000, you should consider working

with a microenterprise service provider. In general, those agencies give training and technical assistance that lead directly to small loans. Most programs include helping you with planning and arranging financial paperwork. (See Chapter Seven, "Microenterprise Lending Programs," for details.)

Organizing financial records. It's to your advantage to know what information about your business the banker wants to review prior to making its loan decision.

If yours is a start-up business, you will not have a company credit history. Therefore, lenders will look at your personal credit background, your current credit character, your business concept, and your financial projections. As your business grows, lenders will require additional information for future loans. Start your business on the right foot by understanding financial fundamentals.

In most cases, the following documents are required by banks from existing businesses:

- Current interim balance sheet and income statement.
- Cash flow projections.
- Pro forma balance sheet and income statement.
- Fiscal year-end financial statements.
- Tax returns for past three years.
- A business plan.
- Current personal financial statement and personal tax returns for past three years (of the owners).

It's a good idea to review all your business records before applying for a bank loan. Doing so helps you assess your future borrowing needs and know where you stand currently. Begin by examining the following:

- Tax records. All records should be available as they currently stand, including notices of past-due taxes and additional assessments, if applicable. Review your records with an eye toward incurring additional costs, particularly if it's close to a quarterly tax payment time.
- Employment records. Trends in employment should be addressed. Are part-time workers hired for seasonal increases in busi-

ness? Will employees be laid off in the near future? Are any employees currently receiving workers' compensation benefits due to work-related injuries? Do you need to pay overtime to complete current contracts in a timely manner? Are all your financial responsibilities to employees and employee benefits current?

- Inventory. Make sure the inventory list is accurate. It should include the name of your suppliers, quantities purchased, purchase dates, prices paid, and the current supply of all in-stock items. Is your inventory sufficient to complete all current contracts? If not, what additional purchases are necessary? From whom and at what price? Are any of those items on back order? Will there be any additional costs for special handling or air freight to complete current contracts?

- Furniture, fixtures, and equipment. You'll find that having separate lists of each category is helpful. Your lists should indicate where the items were purchased, when they were purchased, the price paid for each, and any depreciation incurred. List serial numbers for major items as well. When reviewing fixtures, you should list separately those that are easily removable from those that could not practically be moved to a new location. Are your fixtures security for the lease? Will the fixtures remain with the landlord as part of the lease? If furniture and/or equipment is leased, those contracts should be readily available. What is the remaining term on each lease? What is the buy-out price and the monthly payment?

- Current loan records. At the present time, are there any loans outstanding? To whom is the loan payable? What was the initial loan amount? What is the current balance? What are the terms of the loan? What serves as collateral for the loan?

- Current contracts list. For each current contract, list the total dollar amount of the contract, any deposits or amounts paid to date, the cost to produce each contract, and the anticipated date of completion. How long will the business have to wait to receive payment after delivery? Are any change orders or additions to the contract anticipated? What about deletions?

- Receivables list. What is currently owed to the business? Who owes it? What is the probability that the account will be collected? How long has the bill been overdue? Accounts aging should be listed as past due 30, 60, 90, 120, and so forth, days.

- Payable List. The list should contain each current obligation. To whom is it owed? If the bill was paid on time, would a discount apply? If past due, when was it due? Are there interest or penalties owing? Which bills are disputed? Payable aging should also be listed as 30, 60, 90, 120 days, and so forth, past due.
- Building lease or mortgage. If you lease, list to whom the rent is paid, the date it is paid, and the amount paid monthly. Is there a paid damage or other deposit? What is the term of the lease? Are there any unusual provisions in the lease? What about insurance coverage on the building and on contents? Does the landlord pay the building insurance?

If there is a mortgage, list the date purchased, the amount paid, the monthly payments, to whom it's paid, and the amount of any equity. When was the last appraisal on the property? What kind of loan is on the property? Are there any unusual clauses in the mortgage? Is there a balloon payment due in the near future? What kind of insurance coverage is in place, and what are the limits?

A good deal of time should be allocated to review all of the records when they are assembled and completed. Remember to do a final run-through to ensure that all of the financial data cross-checks and balances and that the information is organized in a logical fashion.

Most importantly, you should thoroughly understand all of the financial material so that you can answer the banker's questions intelligently. This is particularly necessary if your bookkeeper or accountant prepares the material.

Other considerations.   Think through your current and future financial needs *before* seeking a loan. Take the time to understand those needs and establish your priorities. Remember that commercial banks are cash flow lenders. As you ask yourself questions, be sure to think in terms of "cash flow, cash flow, cash flow."

Here are some questions you should ask yourself as you chart your action plans:

Where am I now?   What are your financial strengths? Consider all of the records discussed in the previous section, including cash, receivables, equipment and tools, furniture and fixtures, inventory, real estate, vehicles, machinery, and miscellaneous items of value. (When assigning value to an asset, state cost less depreciation.)

Keep in mind that banks want to know *all* elements of the business. Contingent liabilities play a major role when lenders try to determine what could go wrong with a potential loan. Contingent liabilities are the "what ifs" list of things that could affect your repayment abilities. In addition to evaluating actual debt, banks consider the "worst-case scenario." You should, too. Ponder the following:

- Are there penalties to pay if your current contracts aren't produced on time?
- Will you pay overtime to produce contracts on time?
- Do you owe money for taxes? Is it a current bill, or will there be late penalties?
- Is material kept on hand or ordered on a per-job basis? What is the chance that the cost of materials will be more than anticipated?
- Is the workers' compensation insurance policy current? Are liability and comprehensive policies current?
- Is your company on a COD basis with suppliers? If a receivable is not paid on time, can you buy supplies?
- What is your personal value to the company? If something happened to you, would the company suffer? Are you adequately covered by insurance? Is there a management-succession plan? Is there someone legally designated to take your place if you can't work?
- Do you take home a salary? If not, how long can you continue working without remuneration? What are your personal resources?

As you prepare this information, remember that data should be current within a 30-day time period when they are presented to the bank.

What are my immediate dollar needs? Based on your records, do you need a loan today? Or is current cash on hand, plus collection of current receivables, adequate to pay current bills?

Keep in mind that organizing business records and shopping for a loan commitment take time. Therefore, if you need money now, make some temporary arrangements.

It's not a good idea to begin a new bank relationship when you are desperate. It could cause the banker to question your financial management skills and send up "red flags."

Where do I want to be in three months? Six months? Nine months? One year? Small companies often grow in spurts, then level off. Your business may continue winning new, larger contracts for sales, but not have working capital to produce those contracts. Occasionally, too, an anticipated contract falls through. That leaves a cash flow shortfall that throws off projections. You can more accurately anticipate your future needs by considering two points.

Sales growth

- Examine the business's growth over the past year. Do any patterns emerge that identify either growth or sales decline? Did the company grow steadily each month, or did growth and decline occur in two- or three-month spurts?

- Examine the correlation between last year's sales and the pattern of sales that is demonstrated by current contracts. Does this year's growth follow approximately the same pattern as last year's? Is the percent of increase or decrease in business approximately the same?

- Evaluate the contracts that are pending and estimate those that are expected in the next few months. Does the pattern established by last year's growth or decline and the present business continue in approximately the same percent of growth? If not, how does it differ?

- What part, if any, does seasonality play in the business-growth pattern? Is the business dormant part of the year? Does it require working overtime another part of the year?

- Finally, does the company anticipate expanding the product line or adding a new business location during the next year? If so, what impact will that expansion have on anticipated growth?

Effect of sales on cash flow

- How will the company's anticipated growth over the next 3, 6, 9, and 12 months affect payables, receivables, and the company's need to borrow?

To evaluate potential cash flow, consider:

1. Bulk purchases of goods and material supplies. As sales grow, will suppliers give you discounts if you buy in bulk? Will the cost of borrowing money offset the savings garnered by purchasing in bulk?

2. Large contracts equal extended receivables. As your company grows and wins larger contracts, must you wait 30, 45, or even 60 days to receive payment? Are those contracts larger than before? How does that situation affect cash flow?

3. Supplier credit lines. Will suppliers increase credit lines to accommodate growth?

How can I show creditworthiness? Evaluate your ability to get a loan by examining your business's strengths and weaknesses.

- Business weaknesses:

  Less than three years in business.
  Past-due taxes.
  Lack of profitability.
  Poor bookkeeping practices.
  Slow credit.
  Poor paperwork procedures.
  Limited credit lines with suppliers.

- Business strengths:

  Profitability.
  Adequate cash flow.
  Adequate collateral.
  Good record of receivables collection.

Well-written contracts for sales and services prepared by an attorney.

Good accounting practices.

Good personal credit.

Good track record of customer satisfaction.

Remember, you can overcome most credit weaknesses if you work at it.

What is my contingency plan for loan repayment? Things don't always go exactly as planned. Considering a back-up plan is important.

Demonstrating good financial management skills is essential to every banking relationship. Once you assemble all financial materials for your loan proposal, keep them current.

BANK RELATIONSHIPS

Your business needs require a close working relationship with your lender. However, two situations affect modern banking that make those partnerships more difficult.

Relaxed interstate banking laws made it easier for bank mergers. Many commercial lenders are multilevel corporations with divisions in several states. That means loan approval for your loan may rest with someone several tiers up the ladder who may be unfamiliar with your business.

To maximize bank efficiency and profits, average loan sizes are $100,000 and up. Most small borrowers don't need and can't qualify for those loans.

Keep in mind that money is a product, and bankers recognize the importance of small business lending. Today, many commercial lenders have programs designed for small firms. Others work directly with microenterprise loan funds to assist small borrowers. (See Chapters Five and Seven.) Make some inquiries, and shop around. There are banks that want your business and will work to earn your trust.

Chapter Three

Alternative Nonbank Financing Options

Bank loans are one traditional funding source. Keep in mind, though, that other avenues are open to you.

This chapter gives you a quick review of alternatives. No one option is a panacea. Depending on your business type and growth stage, you can choose a number of financing methods and use them in tandem.

ACCESSING MONEY

Before you consider various funding means, you should know that there are four basic ways you might get money for your business: grants, loans, credits, or investments. All financing methods in this chapter fall under one of these categories. Knowing these alternatives gives you a better perspective when selecting your funding techniques.

Grants

Grants are funds *given* to you. They do not require repayment. For the most part, grants are available only to nonprofit organizations. However, there are specific instances in which grants are available to self-employed individuals and to very small businesses. For example, there are many grant programs in the creative arts. If you are a visual, performing, or folk music artist or writer, it is likely you may qualify for a grant at a national, state, or local level.

Grant programs also are found in other fields such as education, agriculture, and medicine. A limited number of grants are available for innovative research and development for technology-based businesses, too. For the most part, grants are tied to a specific project idea and end with the culmination of that program.

In many instances, the grant application process is a business in and of itself. Grant writing is competitive and time-consuming. Remember, there are many individuals vying for the same funds.

Grant awards can be substantial and worth your time investment. However, each grant has very exacting criteria. It often pays to seek expert advice.

Loans

Money loaned to your business must be repaid under certain terms and conditions specified in the loan agreement. Most loans are tied to an interest rate and time table. Commercial lenders, such as banks and credit unions, rely heavily on your cash flow projections when determining whether or not to give you a loan.

Some loans are collateralized by business assets. However, unless you have at least a three- to five-year track record, it is likely that a commercial lender will expect your personal signature and assets backing the loan.

Historically, many start-up businesses borrowed money for their businesses from friends and family. Others refinanced their personal residences and used the cash received for their business endeavors. While these two avenues are still appropriate options for those who can pursue them, new lending models exist today as well.

Many small borrowers now seek funding from microlenders. These service-provider agencies offer loans to many who would not necessarily qualify through the commercial lending model. Microlenders also strongly consider loans to those who do not have access to money from friends or relatives and may not own a home. (See Chapter Seven.)

Credits

There are many ways a business can improve its overall cash position through credits. While credits do not put dollars in your company, they do free up money you have on hand to spend as needed.

Many municipalities and states offer t[...]
that are willing to locate in specified redev[...]
cases, a tax credit reduces the amount of t[...]
on job training provided and/or the num[...]
within in that geographical location.

If you are considering a new locale for you[...]
idea to investigate tax credits available in y[...] ...ou snould
know that some states also offer additional incentives to businesses
willing to relocate. These benefits are often negotiable based on
your ability to bring commerce to a certain community.

Additional credits are made through trades or exchanges with
other businesses. These bartered transactions might give you printing, equipment, advertising, or other items you need for your business in exchange for your product or service.

When using the barter system, value exchange items at their full
retail price and expect your trade partner to do the same. Keep
good records for tax purposes. Trade-outs are taxable as though
they were ordinary sales transactions.

As a cautionary note, you should establish a barter budget and
stick to it. Bartering enhances cash flow; it should not replace sales
and marketing.

Investments

Small business owners with a unique concept or product might
seek money from outside investors. Generally, investment capital
does not require repayment because investors get stock for their
dollars.

Others are willing to invest in your business if they believe your
idea will be extremely successful. They anticipate a solid return
on their money through your business profitability. To attract investment capital, you must demonstrate a distinctive product or idea,
strong management capabilities, and high projected earnings in a
relatively short time frame.

Investment in your company gives others an ownership position. In most cases, they will want a say in how business is conducted and who manages it.

Occasionally, friends and family members may invest in your
business simply because they believe in you and want to support

ndeavors. A word to the wise: these situations should be
ll thought out and properly documented. It's a good idea as
well to include a buyout provision in your agreement with friends
or family members. If there are misunderstandings as the company progresses, you will be prepared to settle them in a busi-
nesslike fashion.

UNDERSTANDING FUNDING TECHNIQUES

Getting money for your company is further defined through various funding techniques. It's important to understand each funding method, then choose a finance combination that suits your
present needs and future goals.

Each technique has benefits and pitfalls. Some take longer than
others to put into action. While certain funding solutions are inex-
pensive, others can be costly.

A thorough grasp of the mechanics involved helps you avoid
frustrations, time delays, and wasted efforts. Knowing how these
financing techniques work gives you a solid foundation for negotiating the best possible situation for your firm.

Remember, building your company is a long-term commitment.
All businesses need money to grow. Funding knowledge is a valu-
able tool that's worth your time investment, now and in the future.
Review these procedures occasionally for the basics: How does it
work? Who qualifies? What are the requirements and time frames?
What are the pitfalls?

Factoring

Factoring is a method of obtaining quick cash by selling your
accounts receivables at a discount.

Factoring firms do not make loans or advance funds against purchase orders. Instead, they engage in "third-party collection" by
paying you in advance for your receivables and then collecting
their money directly from your customers when the invoices come
due and payable. The difference between what the factor agrees
to pay you and the face amount of your customer invoice is the
"factoring fee."

Traditionally, big factoring companies specialize in volume accounts of $5 million or more annually with emphasis on three industries—carpet, textiles, and furniture. However, as small business plays an increasingly important role in the economy, many mid-sized factoring firms are targeting small business clients in the general products and services sectors as well.

How it works.   Factoring eliminates the "float" between the time you deliver goods or services to your customer and when you receive payment for those goods or services. For example, if you ship your product to your client with a net 30-day bill, you will typically have a 30-, 45-, or even 60-day lag before receiving payment. If you are an established factor account, it is possible to receive 70 percent or more of that invoice within 24 hours.

Factoring can enhance your cash flow. Often, small businesses need a quick flow of cash to offset limitations in supplier credit lines and bank loans. For small businesses that don't have the luxury of a strong capital base to wait out long-term customer payment schedules, sometimes factoring can be the difference between failing and thriving.

Who qualifies for this method.   Most mid-sized factoring firms prefer dealing with a small business that invoices at least $8,000 to $10,000 per month. However, if your company is on a good growth path and has a strong receivables collection track record, it is likely that you will find a factoring firm that is willing to work with you, even though your receivables currently are substantially less than $8,000 per month.

Factors will consider applications from almost any type of small business. The only businesses that are generally excluded are those that produce or distribute perishable goods such as food items.

Small businesses that are likely to be turned down for factoring are those with poor collection records or those in which customers are often dissatisfied or the product or services are of poor quality.

Also remember that your factoring application will be turned down automatically if you have collateralized a loan with a blanket pledge of your receivables. In other words, if another entity holds a first lien right on your receivables, you can't sell them to a third party.

Paperwork required.   The following paperwork usually is required to establish a factoring account for your business:

1. You must complete a basic application, which is a simple document that tells the factor about your business and includes:

    • Name, address, and phone number of the company.

    • Type of product or service.

    • Names of principals.

    • Structure of the company—is it a corporation? A partnership?

    • Brief history of business.

    • Annual gross sales.

    • Receivables collection history.

    • Bank name, address, phone number, and name of your loan officer.

    • Copy of your incorporation papers and a resolution of the board of directors, if applicable.

    • Detailed list of your customers, including:

        Name, address, and phone number.
        Contact name.
        Annual sales volume.
        Account aging record.

2. Some factoring firms may want to see your financial statement and tax returns as well.

Once approved, you will be required to sign a factoring agreement for a specified time. The factor then provides you with an assignment letter that is distributed to all of your clients. The letter informs your customers of your decision to factor your invoices and advises them to make all payments on your account directly to the factoring firm.

Realistic time frames.   If your client records are up-to-date, the factoring firm should be able to initiate its credit checks on your customers immediately. Most factoring firms have computer access to commercial credit information. Depending on the number of customers you select to factor and the availability of credit information on those customers, the realistic time frame to set up your factoring program will probably vary between 2 to 10 business days.

Negotiating the structure of the deal.   There are six important variables to consider in negotiating your factoring agreement:

1. Discount Rate. What will it cost you? Does the benefit you derive from the advance payment offset the cost? Most factoring companies base the discount rate on four variables—account volume, account maintenance, risk, and customer rejection of goods or services.

2. Account volume. How many dollars do you run through the account each month? Obviously, the higher the volume, the more consideration will be given to a lower discount rate.

3. Account maintenance. This refers to how much time the factoring firm must spend on your account each month. If you have repeat orders from the same customers, the maintenance is relatively low.

However, if the bulk of your business is from new clients, the maintenance on your account—the credit checks and collection set-ups—will be high.

4. Risk. This is the estimated difficulty the factoring firm will have in collecting its money from your customers. The better your customers' credit rating and payment history, the lower the risk.

5. Rejection. This refers to the factoring company's estimate of how often your client will refuse delivery of your goods or pay for your services. For example, if you have a strong record of customer satisfaction, rejection as an element of discount rate will be quite low. Conversely, if yours is a new company with little customer satisfaction history, the possibility of rejection will be higher and so may be the discount rate.

6. Percent of advance payment. How much will the factor give you in advance against your receivables?

Advance payments from factoring firms may vary between 50 percent to 94 percent of the face value of the invoice. The most important consideration governing the percentage of advance payment is the specific industry in which you are involved. For example, the construction industry has the highest rate of collection difficulty, and, therefore, most factoring firms will advance only 50 percent of the face value on invoices presented by construction firms.

On the other hand, the trucking industry has an excellent history of customer collection. Most factoring companies will advance up to 94 percent on the face value of trucking contracts.

The balance on your invoice is held by the factoring company until your customer pays the bill in full. Holding a balance on the account gives the factoring firm a cushion against late payment by your customer. Most factoring companies reconcile those balances monthly.

Payment schedule. Upon presentation of your invoice to the factoring company, how long will it take to receive payment? Today, most factoring companies that work with small businesses pay the agreed-on percentage of invoice on the basis of "old line" factoring. In other words, most firms pay within 24 hours of presentation of invoice, provided, of course, that your customer was preapproved by the factoring company at the time the order was placed.

As your small business grows and your cash flow stabilizes, it might be advantageous to progress to a program of "maturity" factoring. With maturity factoring, you are guaranteed payment of your receivables at a set future date, not on presentation of invoices. Therefore, you are still assured of payment, but your discount rate will be substantially lower.

Account selection/rejection. Do you have the right to choose the accounts you wish to factor? How many of your accounts will be refused by the factoring company?

Some factoring firms allow you to select the accounts you wish to factor; while others insist that you present all client accounts—present and future—for their review and possible acceptance.

The factoring firm always retains the right to reject any of your clients, based on their credit history. Some rejections may occur simply because your client is too new in business to have established credit. In any case, you retain the right to contract with your clients that have been turned down by the factoring firm—though it might be wise to do so on a COD basis.

Length of term.   How long will you be obligated to the factoring firm under the terms of your agreement?

In most cases, the factoring company will ask you to sign a contract for at least six months. Because of the paperwork involved, it would be difficult for the factor to justify an agreement for a shorter period.

Recourse.   If the factor advances money to you and is unable to collect from your client, will you be responsible for the uncollected amount?

Remember, factoring is not a loan that has to be repaid. It is the outright purchase of a receivable for a discount fee. However, some factoring firms negotiate their contracts on a "recourse" basis. In that case, you would have to pay the factor any amount that the factor has not been able to collect from your client after a set time.

If at all possible, it is best for you to negotiate an agreement with your factor that is "nonrecourse." What this means to you is that upon acceptance of your client by the factoring firm, the factor is solely responsible for the collection of the receivable from your client. If your client does not pay, the factoring firm absorbs the loss.

Legal ramifications.   Before you sign an agreement with a factoring firm, be sure you thoroughly understand all of the elements of the contract. If you sign an agreement to factor all of your receivables for a period of at least six months, you will not be in a position to assign those receivables for any other purpose, including a bank loan.

Again, the "recourse" issue is an extremely important legal consideration. Be sure you understand your payment responsibilities.

Leasing

Lease financing is a method of obtaining items that are essential to the growth of your business with a minimum initial cash outlay.

Today, it is possible to lease almost anything, including office space, vehicles, office equipment, heavy machinery, furniture, and telephones. If you choose to do so, it is even possible to lease nonessentials, such as art work and plants.

There are two basic types of lease entities—"captive" lessors and "third-party" lessors. A captive lessor is generally a corporation that leases its own product directly to you, the "lessee." A third-party lessor is a company or individual who engages in leasing but does not manufacture or represent a specific product.

How it works.   Leasing is one of the primary financing tools that small businesses can use to extend working capital. Leasing preserves your bank line of credit for other cash flow needs while providing you with 100 percent financing on essential business purchases.

As an example of how lease financing can benefit you, let's say that you need to purchase a sophisticated computer system that will cost $10,000. If you buy that system, your bank might loan 75 to 80 percent of the total purchase price, and you will have to pay the balance—$2,000 to $2,500—up front. If you lease that same system, it will probably cost you the equivalent of two monthly payments—one month plus a deposit—or approximately $400 up front.

Therefore, if you purchase the computer system, it will cost you $10,000 cash out-of-pocket or $2,000 in cash and $8,000 from your bank line of credit. By leasing that computer, your net cash flow savings is $9,600—$10,000 financed less two payments.

When small businesses use lease financing to acquire the business items they need to grow, the bottom-line effect of cash flow can be tremendous.

Who qualifies.   The qualifications for leasing vary from one finance firm to the next. Typically, a leasing company will prefer that you have at least two years in business, strong cash flow history, management expertise, and creditworthiness. However, if yours is a new business, there are leasing companies that will work with you, provided your personal resources are strong and your personal credit is good.

In almost all cases, leasing companies expect small business owners to personally guarantee the lease. Exceptions to that rule would be publicly held companies and small companies with excellent retained earnings and long, strong credit histories.

Paperwork required.   Most leasing companies require the following:

- A lease application, including trade references and bank reference.
- A financial statement.
- An interim balance sheet and income statement, if applicable.
- The history of the business and indication of management experience.

If your business is new, you will also need:

- A personal financial statement.
- Personal credit references.

Once your business has been approved, the leasing company prepares the documentation, including:

- A lease or "master lease."
- The UCC-1 registration form.
- Other appropriate state filing forms.
- A guaranty.
- A delivery and acceptance form.
- Verification-of-insurance form

Depending on the structure of your lease, you may also need to provide evidence of insurance and an equipment maintenance agreement.

Realistic time frames.   If your company has been in business two or three years, has good cash flow, and has easily verifiable credit references, you should be able to get credit approval with most leasing companies in two or three working days. If you are required to provide business financials and/or personal credit information, it may take a week to 10 days for credit approval.

Once your company is accepted, it will probably take the lease company another day or two to complete the proper documentation.

Structure of the deal. Though leasing structures vary from one firm to another, there are a few basic rules that apply universally:

• Economic life. True leases are generally written for a term less than or equal to the anticipated economic life of the item being leased. The Master Tax Guide printed by the Commerce Clearing House is often used to set the standard for product economic life. For example, the guide may state that the anticipated life for an IBM PC compatible computer with X, Y, and Z features is three years. Therefore, if you want to lease that computer, the maximum lease term you could expect would be 36 months.

• Net worth to purchase price ratios. The purchase price of the item you want to lease must be less than your company net worth. A construction company with $100,000 net worth would have a difficult time leasing a $125,000 piece of equipment without backup guarantees and collateral.

• Ownership and depreciation. Almost all leases are written as "leases only" or as "leases with the option to buy." The Tax Reform Act of 1986 states that a lease executed with a specific intent to buy at the completion of the lease term carries the same obligations and benefits as a financed purchase. Therefore, in order to retain tax benefits of ownership, leasing companies do not write leases that guarantee purchase at the end of the term.

• Demonstration of cash flow. You must be able to show the leasing company that your business has adequate cash flow to make the monthly payments over the length of the lease term.

Almost all other conditions of the lease agreement are open to negotiation. One of the advantages of leasing is the flexibility of the structure of the deal to suit your particular needs. Some things that you might want to consider are:

• Selection of lessor. A "captive" lease, or one that is offered by the manufacturer or his designated representative, generally includes insurance and a built-in maintenance agreement. While this may be convenient, it may also be slightly more expensive each month. If you feel you will save money by not having to administer the insurance policy or maintenance contract, a captive lease might be the right option for your company.

A "third party" or "net" lease is one that is offered by an independent lessor. This lessor typically leases a variety of products sold by many manufacturers. In a third-party lease, generally you can negotiate insurance payment and maintenance guarantee issues. You may choose to cover the item under your current insurance policy, furnish the lessor with verification, and assume responsibility for maintenance. On the other hand, you may opt to cover the insurance and service contract within the lease and pay a higher monthly payment.

• Lease versus master lease. A lease is specific to the item you are leasing. All documentation is targeted to that one transaction. However, if you believe you will be leasing other items from the same lessor in a relatively short period, it would be to your benefit to request a master lease. With a master lease, the initial paperwork applies to umbrella-type coverage of most leasable items. Each individual transaction is recorded on a separate lease "schedule." In most cases, a master lease will hasten delivery time and eliminate the need to provide additional documentation.

• Lease or lease with the option to buy. A true lease enables you to use the item you need for your business for a specific time only. This type of lease is most appropriate if your need is short-term or if the leased item is one that is likely to become obsolete quickly.

A lease with an option to buy gives you the right to purchase the item at the end of the term. When writing a lease with an option, there are usually three choices:

1. The purchase price may be agreed to in advance.
2. The purchase price may be a token amount, such as $1.
3. Both parties agree to have the item independently appraised by professionals, and the purchase price is an average of the appraised values.

The option-to-buy purchase formula is reflected in your monthly lease payment. For example, if you negotiate a token purchase price, the monthly payments over the term of the lease will be high enough to recover the lessor's entire investment plus interest.

As a result of the Tax Reform Act of 1986, the impact that leasing has on your taxes is a minor consideration compared to the effect it has on your cash flow. However, as a small business owner, you should be aware of the tax differences between purchasing and leasing. Two items to think about are ownership and expense deduction:

1. Ownership gives you the right to depreciate items on your taxes. If you lease, the lessor—not you—has the right to take depreciation.
2. In most cases, the entire lease payment can be deducted as a business expense. By the same token, if you purchase an item through a bank loan, only the interest and depreciation on that loan can be deducted.

Another thing to keep in mind is that the Tax Reform Act of 1986 makes it more difficult to successfully negotiate a lease with an option to buy. Technically, the IRS considers most buyout options "purchases" instead of leases. They may deny the lessor the right to take depreciation.

Legal ramifications. It is important to note that when you lease, you do not own the property. Therefore, through its legal rights and recourse, the leasing company may quickly remedy problem situations. For example, if a small business owner falls behind on his lease payments, the lessor has the right to seize the property immediately.

Another problem common to leasing is the question of "normal wear and tear." Generally, all leases carry a provision stating that the lessee will return the item to the lessor at the end of the lease term in its original condition less normal wear and tear. Unfortunately, the lessor and the lessee do not always agree as to what constitutes normal wear and tear.

Most leases make it quite clear that the lessee is responsible for insurance coverage. If you allow your insurance coverage to lapse and the lease item is damaged, you are legally obligated to complete the lease payments and replace the lost or damaged item as well.

Professional assistance needed. If you are considering leasing as a financial alternative, it is important to consult your accountant. Together, you can determine the impact leasing will have on both your cash flow and tax situation.

It is also a good idea to ask your attorney to review the lease documents before you sign them.

What it costs.   Monthly lease payments are usually lower than the monthly payments you would incur if you purchased the same item. However, keep in mind that you will not necessarily own the item at the end of the lease term. What you are paying for is the right to use the item for a specified period.

When compared on a dollar-to-dollar basis, leasing is generally more expensive than purchasing an item. Therefore, it is important to assess the overall effect that leasing has on your current cash flow position. An evaluation of that cash flow advantage should be the determining factor in your decision to lease or buy.

Bartering

Bartering is defined as the act of trading by exchanging one commodity for another. While bartering typically does not put actual cash into your company, it does offer you a way to get some of the goods and services you need without disrupting your cash flow. As such, bartering is a financing technique that helps stretch your hard earned dollars.

Bartering can be as simple as a one-time-only transaction between two small business owners or as complicated as a third- or fourth-party, ongoing international exchange.

How it works.   Many small businesses find it useful to trade out some of their goods or services. For example, if a cash-poor carpenter needs advertising to improve his business opportunities, he might be able to trade carpentry services to a local newspaper in exchange for a series of weekly ads. A printer who needs the expertise of a computer programmer to enhance his typesetting capabilities might barter business cards or brochures in exchange for the programmer's services.

There are several different approaches to consider if you decide to pursue bartering for your company.

One way to initiate a barter transaction is simply to determine what product or service your business needs and then find someone who is willing to trade it for your goods or services. Often, trade associations and local chambers of commerce can help you facilitate a trade.

If you believe bartering could benefit your business, it might be best to contact a barter association. There are at least four national computer-based bartering networks, two of which are international in scope. Additionally, there are currently more than 325 local—one office, one marketing territory—bartering groups. Most of these networks are for-profit companies that charge a fee for acting as the conduit in the exchange.

Who qualifies.   More than 20 percent of all business transactions worldwide are conducted through one form or another of trade exchange. As of this writing, 142 countries require some type of "offset" or "countertrade" sale when a product is sold to their nation. Essentially, they will buy only if the seller agrees to purchase or to arrange a third-party purchase of their products to offset their cash expenditure.

There are ample opportunities for small business owners to take part in the barter system. If you have a product or service that is marketable, you qualify as a trade partner.

Paperwork required.   If you decide to initiate a one-on-one trade with another small business owner, the paperwork for that transaction can be minimal. Each party to the trade prepares an invoice indicating the value of the product or service and exchanges that invoice for one prepared by the other party. Differences in value are usually compensated in cash.

If you choose to become a member of a barter association, the paperwork includes:

- A membership application.
- A complete description of your goods and/or services.
- Information on the types of products or services you might be seeking.
- A resolution of the board of directors, if applicable.

Realistic time frames.   If you have never participated in a one-on-one bartering transaction, it might take some time to complete your first satisfactory trade. Essentially, bartering is the fine art of negotiating. But it is complicated by the needs and wishes of a second buyer and seller—your trade partner. Reaching an agreement that is comfortable for both parties is often achieved through trial and error, practice, and patience. However, once you have mastered your bartering technique, you should be able to accomplish your trade-out goals quite efficiently.

If you choose to exchange your goods or services by participating in a local or national barter association, the advantage of computer matching with others interested in trading should help eliminate hit and miss time delays.

Structure of the deal.   Again, there are a couple of options that should be considered. If you are engaged in a transaction with one trade partner, you should expect the following:

- Each party invoices his or her side of the deal at full retail price.
- Any differences in price should be paid in cash.
- If more than one trade is negotiated with the same party or if there will be a series of trades, it is best to agree in advance to settle differences at a prearranged time such as the end of each month.
- Bartering transactions are taxed by the federal government and most state and local governments as cash transactions. Hence, the value of goods or services you receive in lieu of cash is treated as "income," while the value of the goods or services you give the other party is treated as a "sale." Therefore, you must collect sales tax, as applicable, on the goods or services you provide and pay income taxes on the goods or services you receive. To simplify the tax issue, all sales taxes on bartered transactions should be paid in cash.

If you decide to barter on a regular basis through a computerized barter association, you should expect the following:

- Most exchange groups charge an up-front fee to register your membership.

- Once the fee has been paid, your name is placed on the computer for the goods and services you offer, as well as those you are seeking.
- All transactions are monitored through the computer bank; you should receive a monthly accounting of all your barter transactions.
- Trades are recorded in dollar equivalents or "credits." Therefore, it is likely that your trades will be third- or fourth-party transactions, not necessarily one-on-one computer matches. You earn "credits" when a trader receives a service from you, while "credits" are subtracted from your account when you accept service from another party.
- The fees barter groups charge average 8 to 12 percent. Some associations charge a handling fee for each transaction—whether you are buying or selling. For example, one national barter franchise charges 6 percent on a buy and 6 percent on each sell, or 12 percent total. Others charge a fee for only one aspect of the transaction: for instance, 10 percent on sales; buys are free.
- Many exchange associations offer perks similar to other specialty clubs, such as monthly newsletters, special bonus point programs, and so forth.

Legal ramifications. There is one major legal ramification that you should always consider—*taxation.*

- Trade-outs are the same as cash sales and purchases. It is wise to collect all sales tax in cash.
- The goods or services you receive are considered income. If you are a member of an established barter association, that group is required by law to issue you an IRS form 1099-B annually, indicating the trading you completed during the past year.
- If the item or service you receive through a trade-out is a legitimate cost of doing business, you may be able to deduct it as a business expense on your taxes.

Professional assistance. If you are considering using bartering as part of your day-to-day business, discuss the ramifications with your accountant. Together, you can determine how much of your overall income can be based on trade-outs. Your accountant can also help reduce paperwork by designing a simple bookkeeping system for your barter transactions.

What it costs.   If yours is a service business, pay particular attention to the value of your time and expertise. And keep in mind that the your trade partner will most likely invoice you at full retail value for his services.

If your service business is based on your performance alone, you need to budget your trade-outs to maintain an adequate cash flow stream from your other clientele.

If you are planning one-on-one trade-outs, your expenses should be minimal. The major cost is the time it takes to locate willing, acceptable trade partners.

If you are joining a barter association, the initial cost is somewhat more. Fees for the national and international exchanges range from $100 to $700; the average set-up fee is $400.

Partnerships

The right partnership can enhance the small business owner's ability to conduct business and grow. Depending on the structure of the deal, small businesses can benefit from a partnership that exclusively provides funding, or one that also offers shared knowledge and cost distribution on such items as research and development, marketing analysis, and advertising expenditures.

Partnerships can be formed between one or more individuals and/or corporations. That is to say, a partnership is an agreement between two parties, regardless of their legal structures, for anticipated mutual gain.

Partnerships fall into two categories:

1. Joint venture, or "working," partnerships are those in which both parties are active participants. Generally, decisions are made jointly, work is allocated, and costs as well as profits are distributed proportionately between the parties.

2. Limited partnerships, or "silent" partnerships, are those in which one party maintains complete control and liability while the other party receives a predetermined percent of profits for providing up-front financing.

How it works.   Unfortunately, many small business owners consider partnerships their option of last resort. Some of these people have left major corporations to start their own businesses and believe that any partnership arrangement may jeopardize control of their companies.

While the issue of control is an important negotiating concern, in many cases you can enter into a partnership arrangement that gives you the cash you need for your business while maintaining your comfort level as "owner." Partnerships are one form of small business funding in which you can often "have your cake and eat it, too."

Small business owners can find parties that are willing to participate in both joint venture and limited partnership projects. However, in most cases, the partnership arrangement that works best for your business is dictated by the merits of your business today and the perception of what your business can be in the future.

Limited partnerships, which flourished in the late 1960s, 1970s and early 1980s primarily because of "passive loss" tax breaks, have been adversely affected by the 1986 Tax Reformation Act. Though limited partnerships still work as a funding technique, organizers of formal limited partnerships concentrate on businesses that have strong qualifications to attract investors.

However, you can adapt the limited partnership technique in a loosely structured arrangement with "inside investors," such as friends and family members. This funding method works as well for start-up businesses as it does for ongoing companies. In a limited—or, more correctly in this case, "silent"—partnership with friends and family, you maintain full control of your company, handle all day-to-day operations, and return to your investors a predetermined percent of equity and/or profits in your business.

Remember, limited partners are "passive investors" who have no say in business operations.

You should consider a joint venture arrangement if you are looking for "active" partners. In a joint venture partnership, both parties share day-to-day responsibilities. Historically, many small business owners shied away from joint venture partnerships because they felt they had to give up too much. However, today's small business owners recognize that the benefits of shared efforts often outweigh negative preconceptions.

Joint venture partnerships are usually set in motion to produce specific, predetermined results. They can be as simple as an agreement between two small businesses to share office space in order to cut costs for both companies or as complex as a multileveled investment to develop a new technology. Typically, joint venture partners for growing small businesses include:

- Other small businesses. Keeping costs down and productivity high are major concerns of young companies. One way to manage those issues is to participate in joint venture activities with another small business. As an obvious by-product, each company frees up needed working capital by sharing the workload and expenses with a compatible partner.

- Major corporations. Large companies often recognize the important role played by small business in today's economy. More and more major corporations are advancing the notion that joint venture projects with small enterprises are good business. Often, by extending credit and expertise to your company, large firms get more for their dollars than they do by completing the same project in-house. The large company then helps ensure your success—both as a small business and as their future customer.

- Venture capital companies. Small businesses with management "sizzle" or a "hot" product attract the attention of venture capital companies. In addition to providing financial backing, most venture capitalists bring business management skills, contacts, and other expertise to the negotiating table.

Who qualifies.   Because of the flexibility of terms offered by various partnership techniques, all small businesses can qualify for at least one partnership option. The important thing to remember is that you should spend a great deal of time considering the merits of your business, your future prospects, and what you expect from a partnership—before you seek a partner.

Paperwork required.   Of course, the paperwork requirements are dictated by the type of partnership you choose. For example, if you determine that your interests are best served by forming a limited partner relationship with your friends and family, you often sit down together and draft an agreement. The document then is reviewed by the attorneys for the parties.

On the other hand, if you choose a limited partnership with "outside" investors, the paperwork can be quite complicated and must be prepared carefully. Often, the documentation exceeds 100 pages. Items that you can expect to see in an outside-investor limited partnership package include:

1. A business plan with complete financials.
2. An offering memorandum.
3. A partnership agreement, including:

    • The legal responsibilities of the general partners—you, your company, and possibly a professional management company.
    • An explanation of liability limits.
    • The percent of profits (and/or equity) offered to investors.
    • An explanation of accounting procedures and tax structure.
    • Profit distribution projections.
    • Articles or provisions necessary to comply with the partnership laws of your state and appropriate state and federal securities statutes.
    • A "sophisticated" or qualified investor form and investment representation letter.
    • Legal opinions, tax opinions, and further exhibits, including major contracts, business valuations, and so forth.

Joint venture paperwork also varies according to the venture partnership and its anticipated complexity. As in the earlier example, an agreement to share office space with another small business may require only that the landlord accepts both parties on the lease or that one party signs and agrees to sublet to the other party with the landlord's permission.

It follows that if the joint venture project is more complicated, the paperwork will be as well. For example, some required items that you may expect to see in a sophisticated venture include:

- Management and project control agreements.
- Initial funding responsibilities.
- Production assignments—who does what.
- Licensing agreements on any existing or newly developed technology.
- Projected time tables.
- Sales and marketing assignments.
- Accounting procedures agreement.
- Distribution of expenses and profits agreement.
- Dispute arbitration agreement.
- Project close and/or buy-out agreement.

You also can expect that your joint venture partner will want to see your business plan, current financials, any existing contracts that may have an impact on the project, and perhaps one or two letters of recommendation.

Realistic time frames.   The time it takes to complete a partnership transaction is proportionate to the complexity of the deal. Simple transactions are a matter of discussion and agreement, while more involved partnerships may require lengthy negotiation, plenty of paperwork, and a great deal of time.

From the time you submit a proposal, you can expect joint venture negotiations with a major corporation to last from one to six months (assuming your proposal is unsolicited and not a formal bid requested by the corporation).

An outside limited partnership may move more quickly—one to three months—if the paperwork is completed in advance. Under ordinary circumstances, you can expect the process to take one to six months to complete, if not longer.

Timing on partnerships with venture capital firms also varies depending on the thoroughness of your data, timeliness of the project, current availability of capital, and whether the venture firm is pursuing you or vice versa. If a venture firm is pursuing you, it's a safe bet that the firm has already done its homework on your firm and doesn't need to repeat that lengthy process.

Structure of the deal.   The structure of a simple silent or working partnership deal is negotiable. Once the details have been finalized, you should draft the agreement to ensure that all parties clearly understand the duties, obligations, and benefits of the partnership.

Traditional limited partnerships follow a more rigid structure, since they are governed by both partnership and securities laws. Though the rules vary from state to state, you can expect the following:

- You, your company, and/or a professional partnership management firm act as general partners.
- General partners control the operations of the partnership and do so in accordance with the limited partnership agreement.
- In most cases, general partners are also responsible for all liabilities.
- In exchange for investing in the partnership, limited partners receive a percentage of profits that are dispersed according to a predetermined agreement. Sometimes, limited investors also receive an equity position in the company.
- In most cases, the partnership has a specified life cycle and is dissolved at the end of that cycle.
- Usually, at the end of the partnership, you, your company, and/or any other general partners retain ownership of product patent rights, licensing contracts, franchise rights, and all other assets belonging to the partnership.

Limited partners assume a high level of risk when investing in this type of transaction. Therefore, most experienced investors follow their own rigid guidelines when looking for a limited partnership opportunity. The following is an example of some of the qualifications they might look for in a young company:

- At least one year in business.
- Annual gross sales of $500,000+.
- Profit or at least break-even.
- Funds generated should be for second- or third-stage expansion funding.

It is also significant to note that most investors prefer one industry over another. For example, one investor might contribute only
to computer-related partnerships, while another investor might
choose natural resources.

The structure of a venture capital deal is discussed thoroughly
in Chapter Six. However, you should understand that these firms
are in business to finance companies that have the potential to
return approximately 10 times the amount of money invested in
no more than five years.

Legal ramifications.   If you take your time to select a partnership that is right for your business and follow through, you
should have few difficulties. However, there are a few cautions:

• Be clear as to your financial liability in any partnership. In
most joint venture partnerships, each partner can obligate the
partnership with debt. Your responsibilities include all taxes
owed for wage withholding, unemployment, sales, and personal
property of the partnership. Keep in mind that partnership
earnings flow through to the partners and you will be taxed
accordingly.

• Be sure that your agreement specifically addresses dispute
arbitration and disillusionment. How will the partnership end
if things don't go as planned?

• The accidental or premature death of a partner should also
be considered. How will his or her partnership interests be distributed? If the partnership interest flows through to his or her
family, who will handle the day-to-day control of the business?
Could key-person insurance be used to resolve the distribution
of assets upon death of a partner?

• If you enter into a limited partnership with outside investors,
your legal liabilities and obligations to those investors is significant. You should thoroughly understand those responsibilities
before you sign the agreements and be prepared to follow through.

• If you choose to enter a joint venture partnership with a major
corporation or a venture capital firm, you should be very clear as
to who controls the product or technology at the end of the venture.
Do you own the patent rights to items the venture produced or do
they? Who maintains the licensing agreements? Do you have to sign
a "noncompete clause" for further product development in the field?

Professional assistance. There are five types of professionals that you might want to contact if you choose partnerships as a way of generating needed capital.

1. Your attorney plays a key role in forming and reviewing any partnership agreement. If you are involved in a limited partnership with outside investors, you might also need to work with a securities law specialist.

2. Your accountant can help you prepare all the financial materials you need. He or she can also advise you on any changes in your tax situation that a partnership arrangement might dictate.

3. You should discuss your possible partnership arrangement with your banker to learn how the proposed change in your business will impact your banking relationship and your credit line.

4. If you are merging two business enterprises, you may want to contact a business valuations specialist.

5. You may also want to talk to a professional dispute arbitrator. That individual might work together with both parties, so potential partnership differences can be addressed in advance.

What it costs. Of course, your costs vary depending on the type of partnership you choose, the amount of paperwork required, and the number of experts employed. A simple, silent partnership agreement with family and friends could cost as little as one or two hours of your attorney's time to review the document. On the other hand, a formal limited partnership with outside investors could cost as much as 10 to 20 percent of the amount of money raised.

What can go wrong. If you are considering a partnership with family members and friends, keep in mind the adage, "The quickest way to make a new enemy is to do business with an old friend."

Certainly, friends and family often help fund a small business because of personal relationships; therefore, the decision to invest is not necessarily tied to the merits of the enterprise. As the owner of a small business with close, personal investors, you can help keep the financial relationship on course by providing written, concise investment agreements, keeping accurate records, and performing as promised. A thorough understanding of the agreement helps prevent the partnership from going awry; be sure that all the "what ifs" are discussed in advance.

Credit Enhancements

Credit enhancements are assets of recognized value that can be "rented" or borrowed to support a loan or other debt obligation. Essentially, credit enhancements strengthen your asset base so you can stretch your company's borrowing power or guarantee a future payment to a major supplier. As such, credit enhancements are funding "instruments" rather than funding "techniques."

Often, the value attributed to a particular enhancement is based on liquidity and/or stability. In other words, the more liquid and/or solid the asset, the more likely you will be able to use it to secure your debt.

You can get credit enhancements from both individuals and corporations. What you give in exchange depends on their relationship to you and what they perceive as the value of their asset. For example, a corporation may provide you assets in exchange for a percentage of the royalties on a product you are developing, while your mother might loan you her CD simply to help you achieve success.

The following is a list of assets that may be used as credit enhancements:

- Certificates of deposit (CDs).
- Letters of credit (LCs).
- Stocks (usually publicly traded only).
- Insurance.
- Corporate bonds and notes.
- U.S. Treasury bills or notes.
- Lines of credit.
- Trust funds (many are restricted).
- Real estate equity.
- Leases.

- Stored goods of value (in a bonded warehouse).
- Items of special value (i.e., appraised collections of coins, jewelry, art, precious gems, and metals, etc.).

How it works. There are two stages of small business development in which credit enhancements can be particularly beneficial:

1. Start-up. Often when people begin small businesses, they lack the personal asset strength to secure bank loans. In many cases, family members and friends assist by loaning assets to the new company to help increase the asset base.

2. Rapid growth. When a young company experiences rapid expansion, that growth frequently outpaces the ability to support increased bank lines and credit advances from suppliers. To secure credit extensions, small businesses sometimes have to borrow assets or get guarantees from others.

Who qualifies. Credit enhancements bolster your asset base so you can acquire additional debt financing; they do not directly improve your cash flow. Therefore, to qualify for credit-enhancement funding, you need to demonstrate that acquiring new debt is justified by the improved income stream from the loan or credit extension proceeds.

Paperwork requirements. Credit enhancement involves three parties—your company, the person or company providing the enhancement vehicle, and a lender. The requirements of the parties dictate the paperwork. For example, if you negotiate a pledge of a friend's blue-chip stock to help secure your bank loan, you may need the following:

- Your friend might require:

    A promissory note from your business.
    Your personal promissory note.
    A pledge of your shares of stock in the company.

A release of obligation clause from the bank upon the satisfaction of predetermined conditions.

- The bank might require:

An assignment of the blue-chip stock.

Obviously, more complicated scenarios require more detailed documentation. For example, if you use third-party real estate to secure a loan, you might need a current appraisal and title search for the lender and appropriate guarantees for the credit-enhancement provider. For stored goods in a bonded warehouse, you may have to provide proof of content, value, and ownership, as well as all documents pertinent to the collateralization process.

Realistic time frames. Several peripheral factors play a part in defining the time lines for using credit enhancement vehicles. Some things to consider:

- How much access do you presently have to individuals and companies that might have credit-enhancement vehicles?
- How creative can you be in locating those sources quickly?
- If you are recruiting friends and family, what assurances can you give them that your business can repay the loan, thus releasing their collateral?
- If you are going to outsiders, what's in it for them if they help your business? How can you make it worth their while?
- How liquid and/or solid are the assets you might be able to attract? Would your bank or supplier loan against them? Or do you also have to seek out a third-party private lender?

In the best possible scenario—you know someone who believes in you and has a readily available quality asset to loan—the time lines will most likely be determined by your bank's loan approval process. In most cases, you should have an answer within two to three weeks.

On the other hand, in the worst possible case—starting from scratch—you should be able to locate three to five owners of credit-enhancement vehicles in three to four weeks. It might take you another month or two to present your request.

Assuming your company can offer strong assurances of debt repayment and has something of interest to offer, allow three to six weeks of negotiations and contract discussions before an individual or company signs on. At that point, if your bank readily accepts the collateral, it may be another two to three weeks. Realistically, it may take six months or longer to secure that credit enhancement.

Structure of the deal.   Basically, you need to negotiate a deal that is a "win-win" situation in which your business benefits and the other party has a strong incentive.

Sometimes it is best simply to offer that individual or company a percentage of interest for the time you are using the collateral. For example, if your uncle has a one-year CD earning 8 percent annual interest, you might give him an additional 5 to 10 percent interest for allowing your business to use his CD as collateral. If, in fact, you can pay back the loan and the collateral is released, you'll get the loan you need and your uncle gets 13 to 18 percent interest on his investment.

Other times, the individual or company that owns the credit-enhancement asset may negotiate for something other than a higher interest return. Perhaps they may want a percentage ownership in your company or first-right-of-refusal on a product license or patent. To ensure that all parties win in the negotiation, determine how flexible you can be and at what point you'll draw the line.

Once you understand how to use credit enhancements to fund your business, you can be rather creative in structuring deals.

Legal ramifications.   The critical factor in each credit-enhancement deal is whether your company can fulfill its obligations in a timely manner to protect and release the enhancement vehicle.

If you have any doubt, it is best to reconsider the situation. Keep in mind, the goal is to provide each party with a win-win deal. Be careful not to be overly enthusiastic about your ability to repay the loan.

Professional assistance. In most circumstances, you should be able to handle a credit-enhancement transaction with friends or family with little assistance. However, it is a good idea to discuss the potential asset transfer with your bank or other lender first. Your banker can tell you whether the collateral satisfies lending requirements. Once you have the lender's approval, you might ask your attorney to review the documents before you sign.

On the other hand, if you are using an outside party in a fairly complicated credit-enhancement transfer, it's best to discuss the details with your attorney and possibly your accountant before you move ahead. Complicated transactions can affect your legal obligations as well as your bottom line.

What it costs. Depending on the structure of the deal, credit enhancements can be either time-consuming and costly or efficient and well worth the price. If you have to give up too much or if the overall cost exceeds your profitability, it's not the best avenue to pursue.

What can go wrong. Your overall concern will be your obligation to the asset owner. Before embarking, consider every possible stumbling block that could potentially cause a delay in your ability to repay a loan, including:

- Labor strikes.
- Transportation delays.
- Freight damage.
- Back orders of needed materials.
- Workers' sick days, vacations, or unexpected departures.
- Contract disputes with subcontractors.
- Licensing and permit problems.
- Downtime of computer or other needed equipment.

Any of these would be greatly compounded by the payback requirements on the borrowed collateral. If you use "rented" assets, it would be a good idea to extend your planning time for job completion and repayment well past your normal estimates for similar projects.

Franchising and Licensing

Franchising is a method of expanding your business in satellite locations by selling your company as a "package" to other qualified entrepreneurs. That "package" establishes standards for duplication of products and procedures, marketing and advertising identity, hiring and training policies—in short, everything the franchisee needs to replicate your business. In essence, franchising is a way of profiting by sharing your formula for success with others.

Licensing is similar to franchising in that you give others the right to duplicate your technology or service system for a fee. However, when a license is issued, it applies only to a certain segment of your business, not to the business as a whole. Licensees do not necessarily adhere to your business formula or use your name. Instead, they retain the right to incorporate your technology into their existing operations. It should be noted that licenses are usually tied to a specific time frame.

How it works.   Solid franchising concepts and well-defined licensing products can produce enormous revenues for a small business. A clearly defined package is the key to successfully using either technique. You must be able to precisely identify the licensing technology or the elements of the franchise package that can be cloned by others. If your business can accomplish that, you will be in a position to train others to "do what you do" and geometrically increase your profits.

Who qualifies.   Small companies that qualify for licensing generally are those on the cutting edge in their fields. Their advanced products and/or service systems—particularly those that involve expensive or time-consuming research and development procedures—are likely to adapt well to licensing.

Franchising is more encompassing. That is, not only do you have to design and build a better mousetrap, but demonstrate success at managing, producing, packaging, and marketing as well.

Paperwork required.   Paperwork requirements for licensing are not as complex as those for franchising. Typically, for licensing you need:

- A comprehensive business plan. It is important that the plan include an expert evaluation of the technology and/or service system, market analysis, competition comparisons, income and expense pro formas, and cash flow projections.

- Verification of ownership of the technology and/or service system. For example, if you own a patent, copyright, or service mark, you need to make that clear.

- A transfer agreement. This document identifies the technology or service systems that are controlled by the owner as opposed to those that fall under the control of the licensee.

- A licensing agreement. This defines the terms and conditions of the transaction, distribution of funds, timetables, and any restrictions on advertising or marketing.

- An export license. If your licensee is in another country, you may need to apply for an export license with the U.S. Department of Commerce.

Franchising paperwork is comprehensive because a franchisee's earning potential is so dependent on the franchisor. Nationally, franchises fall under the jurisdiction of the Federal Trade Commission. However, many states also have individual franchising requirements.

The following information is usually required to begin a franchise:

1. Comprehensive business plan. The plan must emphasize how the business can be replicated and includes:

   - A complete financial analysis of the company by an outside accounting firm. This review illustrates the financial success and strength of the company. This verification is an integral part of your franchise infrastructure.

   - A market analysis. It predicts your firm's growth potential in geographical areas and takes into account pricing, social attitudes, weather conditions, population clusters, and other elements that might affect your success.

- A feasibility study. This is the final nuts-and-bolts analysis of how you would package your company for others. It typically includes time frames, policies, operating procedures, manuals' development, transfer costs, and so forth.

2. Federal Trade Commission disclosure documents. These include:

- A description of the company.
- A detailed service and/or product delineation.
- A characterization of company management.
- An identification and breakdown of franchise costs.
- A market area description, including franchise sites available and their territory. Any site selection services provided by the franchisor should be indicated.
- Detailed information on assistance provided to the franchisee, including start-up, training, and ongoing updated programs.
- Complete operations and procedures manuals as well as descriptions of pertinent franchise policies.
- An identification of marketing expectations, rules, and regulations.
- A detailed list of franchise equipment, fixtures, or furnishings required.
- A franchise contract highlighting terms and conditions of the agreement.
- Verification of trademark or copyright.
- A list of any adverse circumstances involving the parent company, such as lawsuits or bankruptcy.

Realistic time frames.   Licensing timetables vary depending on the firm's development stage and documentation needed. Assuming you have perfected your technology and/or service system and completed a business plan, it may take about six months to negotiate and close your first licensing agreement. The time may be dramatically reduced if your technology is in demand or if you planned for licensing while completing the research and development phase.

You can expect franchising to take longer. In fact, you might want to allow as much as a year to perfect your package, develop a management and sales team, and complete your registration requirements.

Structure of the deal. The key to both licensing and franchising is clarity. In both instances, your product or service must be clearly defined to structure a deal.

Essentially, licensing is the transfer of technology under specific criteria for a stated time. Licensing programs that are the most successful usually involve technology or service systems that are in demand and that may have taken a long time and a great deal of money to research and develop. For example, a new chemical process that prevents stains on carpets may be in demand by several carpet-fiber manufacturers. Licensees can use the stain-resistant technology developed by the licensor, bypass lengthy research steps, and gain time and cost advantages over their competition.

As the licensor, your knowledge is proprietary; therefore, you should establish the rules. For example, you may choose to license your product for two years and offer it only to companies that sell it outside your marketing territory. You might charge an up-front fee as well as a percent of licensees' profits. At the end of the term, the licensees may have the option to renew their contracts with you, or you might prefer that all rights revert to your firm.

Your negotiating strength will depend on the demand for your product. As licensing technology is very specific, most market niches are limited to a small number of buyers within your industry. That means that the first deal you cut will likely be discussed with other potential licensees. It might be in your best interest, therefore, to establish a license structure right away that suits your future goals and expectations.

Governed by both federal and state regulations, franchise deals usually are more structured than licensing arrangements. Again, the difference is that the licensee buys a piece of your business to improve his own company, while the franchisee is entirely dependent on your success to guide and build his business. Therefore, the structure is legally controlled to protect the interests of the prospective franchisee.

Typically, successful franchise deals have many of the same qualities and characteristics. Some of those are:

- The franchisor has a proven track record. Generally, the company has been in business for three or more years.
- The prototype company demonstrates excellent earnings.Most franchisees seek a 40 to 45 percent annual return on their investment.
- The company package has "sizzle."
- The franchisor is selling a better mousetrap, offering a more exciting product.
- The franchise has a unique visual identity that easily distinguishes it from competitors. McDonald's "golden arches" is a good example. This continuity is recognized in advertising, employee uniforms, and product packaging.
- The prototype company is streamlined. Procedures are constructed so the concept is replicated easily.
- The cost of the franchise is competitive. A franchise might start low—in the $5,000 to $15,000 range—to gain a foothold in the marketplace.
- Corporate advertising, training, and ongoing follow-up add security to the deal. The franchisees feel they can count on the franchisor to support their growth.
- Workable financial packages are available. Often, good franchises cover many start up costs or have a franchisee financing arrangement with a reputable lender.
- Good product/inventory assistance are available. One of the reasons franchises are successful is that the initial package details everything the franchisee needs to make the business work. The franchisor then supplies the inventory at a reasonable price on an ongoing basis.

Structuring a workable franchise package requires effort at every stage, from prototype and planning to start up. However, once a franchise is underway, the franchisor stands to profit enormously.

As a franchisor, you increase your cash flow every time you sell a franchise package. Essentially, you not only derive revenue from the sale itself, but from a percentage of franchisee profits, the sale of products and inventory to franchisees, and from the wholesale price breaks you receive on national advertising, inventory, and equipment.

Legal ramifications. The legal ramifications of licensing and franchising are quite different. As the licensor, you may lose your technology or service system. From the outset, you must define the portion of your product that you are willing to share with others.

With franchising, on the other hand, you have to disclose as much as possible about your business operation and defend the accuracy of any information you give to a franchisee. If you or anyone who represents your company exaggerates the product or its expectations or omits crucial facts, you are legally and financially liable for the consequences.

As a franchisor, you also have a responsibility to uphold any promises you make to your franchisees. For example, if you agree to provide national advertising once a week and on-site training annually, you must do so.

Professional assistance. Both licensing and franchising are highly specialized areas that require expert advice. In addition to the professional services of your accountant and attorney, consider doing the following:

- Hire an outside expert in the field to evaluate your potential licensing technology and/or service system.
- Hire a marketing firm that specializes in selling licenses. In the long run, it saves time and money.
- Before you opt to initiate a franchise, hire experts to review your financial status, your marketing concept, and the feasibility of your package.
- If all goes well, in phase two, you will probably want to hire a franchise consulting firm. Typically, those experts assist in:

  Formulating the concept.

  Streamlining.

  Developing the training, operations, and procedures packages.

  Creating the marketing materials.

Writing the contracts and other disclosure documents.

Filing appropriate legal statements.

Coordinating and negotiating the sales.

What it costs.   Licensing costs vary considerably depending on the experts employed and markets served. Typically, you can expect to spend $15,000 to $25,000. However, if your licensing situation is highly complex, fees could add up quickly and dramatically.

Franchising costs are somewhat more identifiable. Franchise consulting firms usually charge between $25,000 and $50,000, depending on what portion of the work is assigned to them. Often, these firms offset some of their fees by taking a percent of sales. Still other firms collect an initial fee plus a fixed fee for setting up each individual franchisee. Typically, those additional fees range between $5,000 and $7,500 per set-up.

Outside independent experts, such as accountants and attorneys, may charge as much as $50,000, each. Often, these fees are strikingly reduced when services are purchased through a franchise consulting firm.

Some states have legal financial requirements that must be met if you sell a franchise in that state. For example, you might be required to escrow an amount equal to the cost of a complete franchise with the state for a predetermined period of time to give additional protection to potential franchisees.

If either the licensee or franchisee is selected haphazardly, you may lose the revenue stream that could have been generated by a better candidate in a given marketing area.

What can go wrong.   Territories for licensing and franchising should be carefully evaluated, as well. Again, revenue will be lost if marketing areas are too broad.

It might be difficult to exit an unsuccessful relationship. This is particularly true in franchising. State laws are likely to favor the franchisee.

Franchisors usually lose proprietary rights to their products. Both franchisors and licensors lose some control over how their products are used and marketed.

SUMMING UP

Keep in mind that all of these financing techniques can be used in combination. Getting the money you need for your small business requires funding knowledge and appropriate applications. With up-to-date financial records and an understanding of the possibilities, you are always ready to move ahead.

Chapter Four

Investment in Your Business: Venture Capital, Initial Public Offerings, and Other Options

VENTURE CAPITAL

The adage, "Nothing ventured, nothing gained," is an appropriate description of this type of funding. Venture capitalists may be risk-takers, but they know that risk is directly proportionate to the cost of money.

Venture capital is money invested in a high-risk enterprise, usually in the form of an equity purchase, in anticipation that it will be returned for a substantial profit.

Most venture capitalists want to achieve a 20 to 30 percent return on their investment. Because venture capital projects are risky and some are likely to fail, these investors look for projects that, if successful, return 10 times the money invested in about five years.

There are venture capitalists who fit every possible description. Some are wealthy individuals successful in their own businesses, others represent corporations or trusts, and some are groups of investors coming together as an investment company. Venture capital firms often are limited partnerships with life cycles of 7 to 10 years.

Venture capitalists' skills and interests vary as well. Some invest only in industries in which they believe their expertise gives them a significant edge, while others choose to invest in specific geographical areas.

How it works.   Even though there aɪ garding venture capital, here are a few items tᴄ

1. Venture capitalists invest in many small buᴄ a variety of funding levels, such as:

    - Seed capital.
    - Research and development.
    - Second-stage funding.
    - Buyout and acquisition funding.

2. There are more than 600 venture firms in the United States.

3. There are at least 25 state governments that participate in small business venture capital projects.

4. The Small Business Administration (SBA) licenses certain private venture companies as Small Business Investment Companies (SBICs) specifically to invest in small businesses, and Specialized SBICs (SSBICs) to assist socially or economically disadvantaged businesses.

5. More than $2 billion was committed to venture capital funds in 1988, bringing the overall venture total to approximately $30 billion.

With these kinds of statistics, it is clear that venture capital sources are good prospects for small businesses seeking funding.

A point to remember is that most venture capitalists expect an "equity" or ownership position in your company. Therefore, someone else will have an active role in the day-to-day operations of your company. Typically, as each new growth stage is financed, the venture capitalist buys a greater share in your company, and you own less. The theory is that it's better to own a smaller piece of a successful enterprise than 100 percent of an underfinanced, unsuccessful one.

Who qualifies.   Most venture capitalists pay particular attention to your management team. They usually want people leading the company who are experts in their field. While money can be provided to buy equipment, cover research and development costs, and improve marketing techniques, it's quality management that pulls the elements together successfully. It's more likely that your business will qualify for venture capital if your management team is strong and has a proven track record.

Innovative ideas, products, and services that fill a void in the marketplace are also important. Remember, a venture capitalist wants to invest in a company that has the potential to grow substantially in a relatively short time. Your firm should be creative and on the "cutting edge" in your industry if you want to attract the attention of venture capitalists.

Paperwork required. A well-conceived, well-developed business plan is key. It's not necessary to overload your plan with statistics; you can provide that material at the second or third interview. Instead, concentrate on telling the story of the company's development, paying particular attention to the "people power" components that make the business a success.

Keep in mind that your five-year cash flow projections must be strong and realistic and meet the venture capitalist's return on investment expectations.

At the first meeting, a letter of introduction from someone who knows the venture capitalist is helpful. Because most venture firms are inundated with unsolicited requests from small businesses, a personal introduction might help you stand apart from the crowd.

If your company passes the first round of interviews, then be prepared to display the following:

- Complete financials on the company.
- Financial statements for each of the principals.
- Backup data on product development.
- Marketing research completed to date.
- A comprehensive review of the competition.
- Expert opinions, if available and applicable.
- Patent or license documents, if applicable.
- Copies of three years' tax returns, if available.
- Inventory and equipment lists with an explanation of accounting method.
- Outstanding loans and/or line-of-credit documents.
- Copies of any leases or mortgages.

- Incorporation documents, partnership agreements, and so forth.
- Accounts receivable and payable lists.
- Copies of major contracts or letters of intent to purchase your product.
- Any other documents pertinent to your business.

Realistic time frames.   Unless a venture firm was watching and/or pursuing your company for some time, you shouldn't expect negotiations to move quickly. There are two elements that affect the time factor:

1. Because this type of investment is usually high risk, venture capitalists try to minimize that risk by completing thorough due diligence on you and your firm. That process takes time.

2. Venture capitalists want to be both equity and management participants in your business. Therefore, they will take time to get to know you and your associates before making an actual cash investment. Since their participation represents changes for your firm, you will want to get to know them as well.

In light of the risk factors, the due diligence process, and "courtship" time, you can expect the venture capital process to take about six months to complete.

Structure of the Deal.   In most cases, a venture capital deal is one in which a venture firm loans money to the company up-front in exchange for an option to convert that debenture to stock in anticipation of large profits when the company goes public or is sold in the future. Though it is possible to negotiate some variations on this theme, in practice, venture capital projects fairly well follow this precept.

The percent of ownership in your business that the venture firm might want is calculated in a formula that takes the following into account:

- The amount of money needed to achieve the desired results.
- The length of time it will take to achieve those results.

- The annual return on investment.
- The strength of the management team.
- The anticipated funding needs in the future.
- The way and the time to exit the project.

Though the current value of your company is taken into account, venture capital investments are essentially "bets" on future prospects. Therefore, the assets needed for a bank loan, for example, are not as important to a venture capitalist.

As a rule, expect that the venture firm will want at least 30 to 40 percent ownership of your business in the first-funding stage. Of course, as additional funds are needed, you will be expected to give up a larger share of company.

Another part of the deal to be negotiated is the venture capitalist's role in management and/or management decisions. Though some small business owners worry about interference in their business, in most cases, the venture capitalist's involvement can be beneficial to a young company. As previously mentioned, many venture capitalists invest in industries in which they have had some experience. That knowledge, coupled with strong industry contacts, can be as important to a small business as the actual cash investment.

Finally, when considering a venture capital arrangement, think about the end of the deal. You know going in that, at some point, the venture partner will want an exit window. Prior to entering into the deal, take some time to think about your long-term goals and what you want to get out of the venture. Do you want to work hard at your business for five or more years and then sell out? Do you want to consider running a publicly held company? Do you want to become a consultant to your business or to your particular industry? Knowing your goals prior to negotiating the venture will give you confidence and may help set the course for the future of the business as well.

Legal ramifications.   In a venture capital deal you are not borrowing money from a disinterested third party; you are actually selling part of your business.

Your responsibility as the "seller" is to make certain that representations you make about your company are correct. For example, if you owe back taxes and are threatened with a potential lien, you need to discuss it. Or if you are using a patented process but don't own the patent, make that clear from the outset.

Remember, in many cases, the venture capital firm you are working with also has to answer to its outside partners. You can prevent a legal quagmire by being up-front about any potential problems you think your business might encounter.

Professional assistance. Entering into a venture capital deal is essentially equivalent to entering any other type of partnership. In addition to carefully thinking through the positive and negatives, you should consult both your lawyer and your accountant to make sure you fully understand how this change will affect your business.

It is also a good idea to talk over your concerns with other trusted advisors, including your banker, business consultants, and perhaps members of your family.

What it costs. If you decide to pursue venture capital financing, expect to spend a great deal of time working through the process.

You must assemble a complete business plan and provide details about your enterprise and its management. Take great care analyzing the income and expense pro formas; they should project out five years. Your management profile must stand out and demonstrate to the prospective investor(s) that you have the know-how and expertise to make your venture successful.

Next, spend time contacting venture firms and initiating the first round of interviews. This is not as simple as it sounds; it takes a great deal of patience and persistence.

In terms of dollars, some expenses you might incur include:

- Professionally printing your business plan. To attract attention, your presentation should be first-rate.
- Reproduction and mailing costs.
- Building a prototype or gathering expert opinions on your theory.
- A valuation of your business.
- Management profile testing.

What can go wrong. Solid management is what attracts venture capitalists to your company. However, as your business grows with the influx of venture funds, the task of managing a potentially larger company may become more difficult.

As a small business owner, the risk you run in accepting venture capital is that, at some point, your venture partners may not think your experience and performance are strong enough to carry the company forward. It is not probable, but it is possible, that you could work for someone else at the company you founded.

If you decide to pursue venture capital, future funding may create another problem. In almost every instance, growing small businesses need more than one level of financing. If, for any reason, the venture firm opts to end its relationship with you after the first funding round, how will that impact your company?

Finally, it's fair to say that well-run small businesses with their sights set on rapid growth should probably pursue venture funding, but they should do so with realistic expectations. Even though there is approximately $30 billion available through U.S. venture capital firms in any given year, it's certain a log-jam of companies seeking venture funds exists. At any time, there may be as many as 5,000 to 6,000 applicants for each available venture capital slot. The sheer numbers are overwhelming. The process of researching and reviewing proposals is, at best, a time-consuming task for every venture firm looking for a good match.

SMALL BUSINESS INVESTMENT COMPANIES (SBICs)

Through the SBA, the federal government licenses over 200 privately owned venture capital firms that lend to small businesses. Those firms raise their own capital but may apply for an SBA guarantee on a debenture. The debenture, a debt financed by the sale of bonds, is secured by some or all of the venture company portfolio.

The guarantee usually equals the original capitalization. For example, if the SBIC started with $1 million, its SBA guarantee most likely would be $1 million. Depending on performance, this step may be repeated twice.

Most SBICs have selection guidelines similar to other venture capital companies. However, two exceptions apply:

1. SBICs must adhere to the SBA's small business definitions.
2. SBICs may take stock positions, too. However, with a few exemptions, they may not take ownership control.

SPECIALIZED SMALL BUSINESS INVESTMENT COMPANIES (SSBICS)

SSBICs loan to small businesses owned by socially or economically disadvantaged individuals. In exchange, SSBICs get additional government leverage on their debentures.

PUBLIC OFFERINGS

Investment banking firms are the conduit through which individuals invest in publicly held corporations. Essentially, investment bankers make money in two ways—by taking commissions upon placing their clients' buy or sell stock orders and by bringing new corporate stock issues "public."

If your company chooses to go public, there are a series of steps you must take. This process moves your business from a closely held firm to one in which anyone may purchase stock.

Usually, an investment banking firm is selected to "underwrite" or manage that procedure. Here are some things an underwriter might do for your emerging company:

- Assist in locating "seed money" or money needed to cover the costs of going public.
- Help prepare entrepreneurs for the public process.
- Arrange a due diligence meeting to formally present the small business owner and the company to the stock brokerage community.
- Establish a network of stock brokers to syndicate the new stock issue.
- Bring its own group of investors into the deal.

Often, before a company takes the public offering step, it raises funds by making an intermediary move. This is done by selling a smaller amount of stock to a select group of investors called "insiders." This middle-tier financing has several functions. For example, it:

- Supplies the company with transitional working capital.
- Provides funds to clean up payables to give the company a better footing.
- Gives family members, friends, and loyal employees the opportunity to purchase stock at a lower, first-round financing price.

This first funding step is generally presented to insiders in the form of a "private memorandum" document. The memorandum details the purpose of the offering and funds dispersal and acknowledges early-stage investment risks. Though inside investors purchase their stock at much lower prices, that stock is "restricted" or nonnegotiable for two years to protect both the company and the public.

Some small firms choose to sell stock to insiders without completing the public offering step. There are benefits and pitfalls. To the good, those companies raise money they need immediately and have fewer stockholders. The downside is that these companies:

- Spend comparatively more for investment banking and legal services.
- Contribute many personal hours selling the concept.
- Must answer to stockholders who are holding their stock for the future.

How it works.   There are a number of ways that a small business owner can benefit from an association with an investment banking firm:

1. Investment bankers often have excellent contacts in the venture capital arena. A personal introduction to a venture capitalist by an investment banker could certainly be to your funding advantage. Some investment banking firms even have their own venture capital programs to encourage emerging young companies.

2. Though your company may not consider going public now, it may in the future. An early association with an investment banking group gives you an opportunity to learn the process without the pressure. It also lets the investment banking group know your firm and offer suggestions to guide your future. If you choose to go public at a later date, the investment banker's early guidance will put you a step ahead of the competition and probably save you time and money.

With or without contacts in the investment-banking community, a young company may pursue funding by selling stock through a private-placement memorandum. In fact, the sale of stock through private offerings is one of the most common ways small businesses obtain private investor funding. (See "Professional Assistance Needed.")

In 1982, the Securities and Exchange Commission (SEC) adopted "Regulation D" as part of the Securities Act of 1933. Regulation D explains the rules—504, 505, and 506—under which certain stock offerings are exempt from federal regulation. These exemptions, though restricted to specific dollar ceilings and investor qualifications, give young companies flexibility to sell stock privately to investors without going public.

Who qualifies.   When seeking a public offering candidate, most investment banking firms seek the ideal. They look for a growing small business that is at least three years old and has excellent management, a great product, annual earnings of about $1 million and growth of about 20 percent per year.

Although some small companies are exceptions to the rule, most young businesses are not candidates. For example, if your company produces a revolutionary product with vast marketing potential or if your company's management team has a track record in taking a company public, you might be a likely candidate for a public offering bid.

Paperwork requirements.   Public offerings require an enormous amount of documentation. Experts must prepare much of it. A sampling of some of the documents you will need to go-public include the following:

1. A "registration statement" must be filed with the
    Securities and Exchange Commission. This document
    contains two key parts, the prospectus and a supplemental
    information section.

    • Prospectus—provides investors with information and
      required legal data. It helps contributors determine
      whether or not they will invest in the company.
    • Supplemental—contains additional information, such as
      pertinent charts or statistics.

2. Agreements specific to the underwriting, such as contracts
    with:

    • Accountants to perform an audit.
    • SEC lawyers.
    • A selected investment banker.
    • Assisting underwriters.
    • A transfer agent.

3. A questionnaire for officers and directors of the company,
    detailing personal and business financial history.
4. The "Blue Sky" memorandum, which permits you to sell
    stock in other states.
5. An audited financial statement.

The documentation for a private memorandum stock offering
is less complicated, but should be prepared diligently to protect
the company. (See "Legal Ramifications")

The principal instrument set forth is the memorandum itself;
however, you need to compile other company documents to accurately prepare the memorandum. That information includes:

• A description of the offering, including purchase price,
  number of shares, commissions payable, and so forth.
• The history of the company.
• Company product(s).
• Management profiles.
• Board of directors' profiles.
• Aggregate compensation for top management and annual
  compensation of officers and directors.

- General market information.
- Competition and present and projected market share.
- Special considerations, such as government regulations that might affect the market.
- A description of company facilities.
- The use of proceeds.
- Stock dilution factors (refers to investment tiers).
- A description of the securities offered, including voting rights, liquidation, dividends, restrictions, and so forth.
- Real and anticipated risks.
- Selected financial information.
- A list of officers, directors, and all people owning more than 10 percent of the company's stock, showing number of shares and percentage of ownership.
- A stockholder's subscription agreement.

When the document is completed and you are ready to begin selling, your attorney will also have to file Form D with the Securities and Exchange Commission.

Realistic time frames.   If you are thinking about taking your company public, you might want to allow one to two months to get your files in order, select the underwriter and SEC attorney, and file your registration statement. Then add on another 30 to 60 days to receive and answer comments from the SEC. The actual offering should take about two more weeks. The approximate total time element is 90 to 120 days. It is not unusual, however, for an offering to drag on due to a number of factors, including the upfront compilation of proper paperwork.

A private memorandum may take two to four weeks to prepare, depending on the accuracy and availability of your data. In most instances, a private memorandum states that the company has 90 days to sell stock, usually with a 30-day extension provision. Of course, if the officers and directors can sell the stock quickly, the offering can close sooner.

Structure of the deal.   In most public corporations, there are usually several tiers of stock ownership. The first level consists of the founders of the company. The second tier comprises insiders—family, friends, and employees. The third stock level typically is purchased by the general public.

The structure of a public stock offering can be further complicated when stock is sold as either "common" or "preferred." More than one private memorandum can be issued, and "warrants"— options to purchase more stock at a set price in the future—may or may not be attached to the offering.

"Dilution factors" are other important structural considerations. Dilution is tied to initial stock pricing and directly affects percent of ownership as the company moves from private to public.

Original owners maintain large blocks of stock, and ownership control, because per-share stock prices increase as the stock moves into the public arena. Initially, the appraised value of the company's total assets prior to going public is divided by the total number of stock shares allocated by the board of directors. That determines the first price paid for the stock. Once the company is public, market demand for the outstanding shares controls the price.

The following example illustrates how a company's stock typically might be priced as it moves from private to public:

Owners/founders of the company purchase $1,000 of stock at $.01 per share = 100,000 shares.

Family/friends/employees, insiders purchase $1,000 of stock at $.05 per share = 20,000 shares.

The general public purchases $1,000 of stock at $.25 per share = 4,000 shares.

Fluctuations in the stock market also affect the structure of the deal. When the market is strong and the chances of successfully taking a company public are good, then you will want to move quickly to take advantage of the "window." However, if the market takes a downturn and the window closes, it is probably best to postpone the deal.

Many factors change the structure of a public offering. If going public is an option, you should review some actual cases of public firms similar to yours prior to charting your company's course of action.

By comparison, a private-offering memorandum is less complicated. Once you decide to raise capital by selling stock in your corporation, you'll need to do the following:

- Determine how much money you want to raise within the boundaries of the 504, 505, or 506 exemption.
- Determine how much ownership in the company you will give up.
- Have your SEC attorney prepare the memorandum and file regulation Form D with the SEC.
- Ask your attorney to review with you, your officers, and directors all rules for selling stock under the appropriate exemption.

Most private stock offerings are sold on a "minimum/maximum" basis. In other words, money obtained from the sale of stock is held in an escrow account until the stated minimum is reached. At that point, your company may break escrow and spend the money even if the maximum is never achieved. However, if you do not sell the minimum amount in the specified time, money in the escrow account is returned to the investors and the offering is closed.

Legal ramifications. Public offerings are complicated. They require a great deal of study and counsel. As a public company, your firm has a responsibility to uphold the public trust. That becomes your primary consideration. To do so, you must comply with all aspects of the laws regarding the protection of your stockholders.

Legal ramifications for violating the letter of the law are severe. It should be noted, too, that ignorance of the law is not an acceptable excuse for wrongful action.

If you choose to raise money by selling stock through a private memorandum, you must also adhere to laws that protect your stockholders. For example, you must hold annual meetings to elect directors and keep your stockholders up-to-date. Under certain prescribed circumstances, stockholders have the right to examine your books. In addition, you are always obligated to inform your stockholders of any major change in the status of your company.

Professional assistance needed. You should engage an SEC attorney if you pursue either a public offering or a private memorandum. You need help from your accountant, as well. In some cases, you might hire an accounting firm that specializes in public offerings and/or audits. If you decide to go public, you will want to sign with a reputable investment banker.

What it costs. Public offerings can be expensive, especially for a firm that is raising less that $1,000,000. As a rule of thumb, the investment banker will want 7 to 10 percent of the amount of money raised. You will likely pay the underwriter another 10 percent or more in additional costs, including legal fees, accounting fees, printing fees, filing fees, and out-of-pocket expenses.

The costs tied to a private memorandum usually include:

- An attorney's fee—normally $5,000 to $15,000.
- Accounting fees, as required.
- Printing and mailing expenses—$1,000 to $2,500

What can go wrong. A public offering is something akin to juggling dishes in the air while balancing on a bouncing ball; almost anything can go wrong. Each and every decision you make will significantly impact the next.

Assembling an expert team is your best defense against major catastrophe. Always present your company and your case truthfully. Wait for market conditions that provide a window of opportunity.

If you decide to use a private memorandum to raise capital, there are a few potential problems that you should keep in mind.

1. If you set your minimum dollars to break escrow too high, you run the risk of not completing your offering.
2. If you set your minimum too low, you may find that investors are leery and might want to hold out for a "last in" position.
3. Remember, stockholders tend to get edgy if they don't know what's happening. Keep them informed, regardless of whether the news is good or bad.

4. All pertinent information about your business must be covered in the initial memorandum. If you omit important facts, you might face a potential lawsuit.

Public offerings are not impossible. However, it is important to reiterate that any offering is a major responsibility and should be undertaken with an extraordinary deal of forethought, expert advice, and planning.

As the management team of a publicly held company, you and your colleagues will experience major changes in the way you do business. Literally, your business life becomes a fishbowl. For example, your salary and compensation package, plans for new product development, and day-to-day operations are open to public scrutiny.

If all the indicators suggest going public is the right choice, do so, but do it understanding fully your obligations and new challenges.

FOREIGN INVESTMENT

Foreign investments in U.S. small businesses tend to follow the partnerships and venture capital models previously discussed in this book.

Like American venture capitalists, foreign investors tend to invest in their specific fields of interest and at funding stages that make them most comfortable. As with a U.S. partnership, foreign parties look for partners with whom they can form successful, mutually beneficial ventures.

Foreign investors look for businesses that are developing new products, technology, and/or service systems. By funding or partnering those developments, the investor corners the future market for those goods in other countries.

Sometimes a foreign investor works with a U.S. company that has a notable existing product. While the U.S. market may have reached saturation, the product might have enormous potential when exported.

Generally, foreign investors are not looking to invest in American companies whose products are sold only in the United States.

One of the great benefits of working with a foreign investor is the help your firm gets in learning about and penetrating new export markets.

How it works.   In many instances, a foreign investor might consider working with a business that U.S. investors think is too young or too small. (Japanese investors are a noted exception, as they tend to look for companies that are in the second or third development stage.) Remember, most foreign funders are in for the long haul. They will have a vested interest in bringing along new companies that give them future export edge and exclusive foreign marketing rights.

Market research is one key to finding a foreign investor for your business. Verifying product marketability is time-consuming, however, it will help you determine whether or not a foreign partnership or venture will work. Research also helps you geographically narrow down your investor search, particularly if exporting looks feasible only in certain countries.

Who qualifies.   Much like attracting U.S. venture capital, you must have a product that investors think has "sizzle" and good market potential. Usually, you must be willing to export your product. If real property is a key to your success, it won't be exported, but the management style might be duplicated in a similar project and personnel might be exchanged. All other qualifying criteria depend on the individual investor's needs and how comfortable the two parties are with the match.

Paperwork required.   A simple, well-written business plan is essential. The executive summary is particularly important. Care should be given to a thorough discussion of company-management skills. As most foreign investors take a passive role in your company, they expect top-notch management. Financial pro formas should be comprehensive and extended for five years.

You may also find you need new letter-writing skills. Your initial contact and most follow-ups with many foreign investors will be in writing. It is important to recognize and follow correspondence customs of that nation when writing to an investor in another country.

Depending on the structure of the deal, other paperwork will be required. For example, if you agree to a partnership, you will need to complete partnership documents. If you choose a venture relationship, those paperwork requirements will have to be fulfilled.

As you are negotiating the deal, you will want to check with the nearest U.S. Department of Commerce office to make sure your product conforms with current trade policies. Remember, certain technologies are restricted from export to some nations. Early on, you need to know if your product requires a "general" or a "validated" export license and if trade is prohibited with any countries.

The Department of Commerce office can mail a copy of its Commodity Control List to you. That list details various goods and technologies and indicates the classification. For example, if you produce certain aircraft computer software, the list might tell you it can be exported to some nations but not to others.

If you have difficulty ascertaining the category for your product, write a short description, attach specification sheets, and mail that to the Office of Export Licensing. A qualified engineer will review your materials and advise you of the appropriate license classification.

In addition, specific paperwork is required by the foreign investor group. Their home nation might want other documentation.

Realistic time frames. Typically, timetables in other countries tend to be less hurried than in the United States. Foreign investors look for long-term relationships. Loyalty and commitment are very important, too. Therefore, it's quite likely a foreign investor will take time evaluating you and your firm before making a final funding decision.

Additionally, you need extra time to learn the customs of your foreign investors, the nuances of their language, and the differences in management style. It's likely you will be expected to visit their country once or twice, too. If you pursue foreign investments for your firm, you should count on at least a year, perhaps two, to develop those relationships.

Structure of the deal. Funding deals with foreign investors can take many forms. For your convenience, a few options are listed here:

1. Venture capital investment. It's likely this structure closely follows U.S. venture deals. That is, up-front the investor wants 30 to 40 percent interest in the company and a say in policy decisions. Management expertise is important to the investors as it is not likely they will participate in day-to-day operations.

   There are some ways in which foreign venture capitalists might differ from their U.S. counterparts. For example:

   • Export product marketability is a key factor.
   • The right to represent those products in foreign markets is important.
   • Some foreign investors want licensing rights to current and/or future technological developments.
   • If your product or service system is particularly interesting to a foreign investor group, it is possible they will want you to move your operation to their country—lock, stock, and barrel.

2. Partnerships. Again, many of the characteristics of U.S. partnerships will apply. (See Chapter Three, "Alternative Nonbank Financing Options.")

3. Some other structures you might find include:

   • Export brokers. Essentially, these are trading wholesalers that buy goods directly from U.S. manufacturers to sell in other countries.
   • Foreign trade companies. These companies market goods, and sometimes services, overseas. Most of the time, they accept the goods on consignment; occasionally, they buy goods outright. Many foreign trade companies have offices throughout the United States.
   • Trade partners. Many small businesses coventure exports with larger U.S. companies. These bigger firms usually have international experience, contacts, and financial wherewithal. Some also have excellent track

records in third-party trading. That is, they might exchange your goods for another product and then sell that product to another nation to pay you in cash.

Legal ramifications. When you do business with someone based in another country, there are some inherent problems with the deal. Some things that you might want to consider include the following:

- Language, customs, and other cultural differences affect the way each party understands and interprets the agreement.
- Proper documentation must be in order and kept up-to-date.
- You and your investor should agree on marketing policies and customer contract verbiage, in advance, to prevent quarrelsome legal delays.
- Account collections in foreign countries could be tricky. You might want to investigate trade insurance or secure internationally acceptable letters of credit to guarantee payment.

What it costs. To a great extent, the cost is tied to the type of funding negotiated. However, there are some specific costs you could expect in any foreign investment project. Those include:

- Travel expense. Probably, you must make at least one trip. It is possible your investors will want you to stay in their country for an extended visit.
- Translation, fax, and telephone costs. When you negotiate with a foreign investor, you make many phone calls and exchange lots of paperwork. It's likely you will get documents translated, too.
- Legal fees. Before you complete the deal, there may be more legal fees than you would ordinarily anticipate in a similar U.S. transaction.
- Time. Your time investment will be significant. Generally speaking, negotiations move very slowly. You should be prepared to devote a good deal of time to working through the process.
- Currency exchange rates. These may vary from the time you initiate the transaction until you complete it. A dramatic change in rate could be very costly.

What can go wrong. Misunderstandings are one of the greatest problems with this transaction. You must muster a good deal of patience to work through those frustrations.

Getting banks to back you once you have secured an order is another common dilemma. Hopefully, your foreign investor can secure the purchase order with an acceptable letter of credit or help you obtain the appropriate insurance.

Identifying true investor sources is complicated. Because of language barriers, it is fairly easy for "middlemen" to control the negotiation process—at your expense. Often, these brokers misrepresent their role—sometimes accidentally, sometimes not. It's in your best interest to perform your own due diligence on intermediaries and your potential partner.

THINK ABOUT IT

You should take careful consideration before using any of the financing techniques in this section. In each case, you give up at least partial control of your company in exchange for funding. Sometimes, selling all but a small percentage of your company might be worthwhile. Other times this may not feel comfortable.

Chapter Five

Federal Governn
Sources

A plethora of federal grant and loan programs is set up to help specific, targeted small businesses. These programs are available through various government branches, such as the Defense Department and the Commerce Department.

You must apply for these programs directly. Each separate federal agency has a liaison officer and accessible printed project information. In total, there are approximately 1,200 ventures budgeted annually.

Keep in mind that these grants/loans are quite specific. Though winning a project makes your efforts worthwhile, realistically, you could devote a great deal of time searching out the right program. A complete listing of most funding obtainable through the federal government may be found in J. Robert Dumouchel's GOVERNMENT ASSISTANCE ALMANAC, published by Omnigraphics, Inc., in Detroit and Foggy Bottom Publications in Washington, DC.

SBA FUNDING OPTIONS

Basic loan programs established by the Department of Commerce's Small Business Administration (SBA) are applicable to almost any small firm. The SBA, started by Congress in 1953 to protect and assist small business, makes an effort to provide funding that serves entrepreneurs' changing needs.

SBA lending programs modify and expand over the years to better facilitate the public. From time to time, certain programs that have become obsolete are dropped. In their place, new, creative programs are initiated. The principal mission of SBA lending is to facilitate borrowing for small firms that cannot obtain funds from conventional lenders on reasonable terms without assistance.

...ntly, the SBA offers several options to assist small busi-
...sses. In most cases, loans are generated by private lenders and
guaranteed by the SBA.

You can get paperwork for an SBA loan from your local SBA office or from a participating bank lender. In any one given locale,
generally 80 to 95 percent of all banks use the SBA loan guarantee
programs. Your SBA district office can give you a list of the most
active SBA bank lenders in your area.

In most regions, once the SBA receives completed paperwork,
a decision on your loan is forthcoming in a matter of 10 to 14 days.
As a cautionary note, however, it could take some time for you to
compile all the necessary documentation unless you prepare it
prior to shopping for a loan. (See Chapter Two for loan-readiness
guidelines.)

Preferred Lenders

Certain banks within each state qualify as preferred SBA lenders.
These banks usually demonstrate a willingness to promote small
business lending and write many SBA guarantee loans. Because
they have demonstrated experience, a preferred lender can ap-
prove a loan guarantee without submitting loan documents to the
SBA office first. If you have an established working relationship
with one of these banks, the bank's preferred status may save you
a little time.

On the other hand, you should know that a preferred lender is
only authorized to provide up to a 75 percent SBA guarantee against
your loan without submitting documents for prior approval. That
has three possible effects on you as the borrower. Your creditworthiness must be a little stronger. You may qualify for a slightly
smaller loan. Or, to get the maximum guarantee, you should ask
the lender to submit the loan to the SBA for approval and wait out
the 10 to 14 days.

Your local SBA office can give you a preferred lender list.

7(a) Guaranty Loan Program. Most small firms qualify
for funds under this program, though certain limitations do
apply. The agency can guarantee up to 90 percent of a loan under

$155,000. It guarantees up to 85 percent on approved loans exceeding $155,000. The maximum amount the SBA can guarantee is $750,000.

The loan term cannot exceed 10 years for working capital and 25 years for fixed assets. Lenders cannot charge more than 2.75 percent over the prime rate on loans guaranteed by this program. As a caution, it's important to keep in mind that the average small business loan guaranteed by the SBA is $175,000 and the average maturity is eight years.

Low Documentation Loan Program (LowDoc).   The Low-Doc program reduces paperwork required for 7(a) loan requests less than $100,000.

The focus of this loan is on character, credit, and experience. The SBA provides a one-page loan application. You fill out side one and the lender handles side two. In most cases, you will receive an answer on your application from the SBA in two to three days.

The SBA guarantees up to 90 percent of the loan. As with other 7(a) loans, adequate security is required. Business assets are used for collateral, and personal assets are sometimes pledged, as well. Your personal guarantee and that of other principals are needed. Eligibility includes those starting a new business.

Keep in mind that the LowDoc Program is administered through your bank. Your lender may require additional paperwork and specify collateral. Loans over $50,000 must submit three years' corporate tax returns or a copy of Tax Schedule C.

Greenline Program.   This SBA procedure offers short-term, cyclical, working capital loans to small companies. The program helps owners level out cash flow during periods of rapid growth and/or seasonality. Here are two examples:

Consider a typical garden center. In most U.S. regional climates, a gardening firm does most of its business in late spring, summer, and early autumn, but would expect business volume to decline during the winter. Thus, the company could experience seasonality cash flow difficulties and anticipate borrowing during those cold months.

On the other hand, a manufacturer may maintain a steady cash flow producing 150 widgets each month. However, if the company gets a large contract to produce 300 widgets in one month, the owners might need extra cash for labor and materials.

While these two companies are quite different in nature, each needs money for a specific purpose during the ordinary course of business.

If you are applying for a loan under the GreenLine Program, generally, loan advances are made against your certified level of inventory and accounts receivable.

SBA regulations governing the 7(a) Loan Guaranty Program also apply to the GreenLine procedure.

Vietnam-Era and Disabled Veterans Loan Program. Vietnam-era and disabled veterans who are not able to secure a loan through private sources can turn to the SBA for help. When possible, loans are guaranteed through commercial lenders on a 7(a) loan basis.

However, for those veterans who cannot qualify through this program, the SBA will acquire financing for eligible veterans interested in starting a small business or expanding an existing one. These direct loans carry a maximum loan amount of $150,000.

Handicapped Assistance Loans (HAL). Physically challenged small business owners and private or public nonprofit organizations that employ handicapped individuals or work on their behalf can obtain financing under this SBA special loan fund. Borrowers may use proceeds for starting, acquiring, or operating a business.

Under the HAL-1 program, the SBA guarantees up to $750,000 through commercial lenders to nonprofit organizations that function on behalf of disabled individuals. Only state and federally chartered groups qualify. Borrowers must show proof that they operate for the benefit of the handicapped.

Handicapped individuals may apply for funds under the HAL-2 program. Applicants must provide evidence that the business is qualified, for-profit, 100 percent owned, and actively managed by one or more handicapped individual(s). When possible, the 7(a) loan program is used. However, the SBA can also make direct loans in amounts up to $150,000.

7(m) Microloan Demonstration Program. Small firms needing less than $25,000 may qualify for funding from this process. The MicroLoan fund is uniquely beneficial to self-employed individuals and home-based businesses.

There is no loan minimum: it may be as low as a few hundred dollars. The emphasis of this relatively new program is on providing employment, addressing community needs, and improving the overall neighborhood. Entrepreneurs may use proceeds for purchasing machinery, equipment, furniture, fixtures, inventory, supplies, and working capital. Funds may not be used for debt payment.

The SBA MicroLoan program is administered by local nonprofit organizations. In addition to making loans, these groups frequently offer technical assistance services as well. Contact your local SBA office for the names of organizations paricipating in this lending program. (See Chapter Seven, "Microenterprise Lending Programs.")

Disaster program. When the president of the United States declares certain designated areas of the country as "disaster areas" due to natural disasters such as fire, floods, earthquakes, tornadoes, and hurricanes, the SBA is ready with special assistance.

Physical damage loans. These loans are made to uninsured firms needing to repair or replace damaged buildings. Proceeds may be used to obtain predisaster condition for fixtures, inventory, equipment, and leasehold improvements.

The loan ceiling is $1,500,000. Loans are disbursed through disaster assistance centers to qualified applicants of businesses and nonprofit organizations.

Economic Injury Disaster Loans (EISL). These loans are made to businesses suffering downtime while their businesses are inoperable. Loans funds are used to replace working capital that would normally flow through the business had the natural disaster not occurred.

Both of the above loans have low interest and generous term repayment plans. When a disaster happens, the SBA establishes on-site offices staffed by experienced teams to assist victims with timely loan processing and funds dispersement.

Small Business Investment Companies (SBICs). See Chapter Four, "Investment in Your Business: Venture Capital, Initial Public Offerings, and Other Options."

Women and minority business ownership. Helping minority and women-owned businesses get started, expand, and stay successful is a major goal of the SBA. Historically, these two groups have had a difficult time accessing loans and garnering markets for their products and services in the traditional business environment.

In 1978, Congress approved a capital ownership development program for minorities. Under this program, SBA staff work with members of local community development agencies and individually with minority business owners to help them become successful.

An ongoing women business ownership program began in 1977. In 1983, the SBA initiated a series of training seminars and workshops specifically targeted at women who wanted to own their own businesses.

For information on either of these programs, contact the Woman Business Owner or Minority Business Owner agent at your nearest SBA district or regional office. Note: A minority or woman-owned firm is defined as one that is at least 51 percent owned, controlled, and operated by a minority or woman.

8(a) Minority Small Business Contract Set-Aside Program. Annually, the federal government spends millions of dollars on contracts for goods and services from the private sector. Through set-asides, this program assures economically and socially disadvantaged businesses a fair portion of those contracts.

Qualified small firms receive management and technical assistance, as well. Contract financing is also available.

8(a) Participant Loan Program.   This program makes loans available to those small firms participating in the 8(a) federal contract plan. Commercial lenders can disburse these loans via the 7(a) Guaranty Loan Program. The SBA can also make direct loans to qualified business owners who contract with the federal government. Borrowers may use proceeds for buildings, working capital, or equipment.

Women's Prequalification Loan Program.   The SBA inaugurated this program in 1994 to aid women business owners. The purpose of the procedure is to preapprove women business owners for an SBA guaranty loan prior to their asking a bank for a loan.

This program cuts through red tape, giving women applicants a fast answer to business loan requests of $250,000 or less. Approved loans are worked through commercial lenders via the 7(a) Guaranty Loan Program.

504 Certified Development Company Program (CDC). Loans under this program are made by specific companies approved by the SBA for the purpose of promoting economic growth in both rural and urban areas. Job creation and retention are the standards by which growth is measured.

To qualify for funding through this means, a small firm must use the proceeds for plant construction, acquisition, conversion, expansion, and/or for the purchase of machinery and equipment. Funds may not be used for working capital.

The minimum 504 CDC loan is $125,000. Typically, there are three partners in the loan. Most often, a private lender provides a first mortgage for 50 percent of the loan. The SBA 504 CDC lender provides a second mortgage for a 40 percent guaranteed debenture by the SBA on a total loan commitment of no more that $750,000. The borrower is then required to contribute the remaining 10 percent.

However, there are exceptions to this loan structure. If the CDC lender has great confidence in the small company, on occasion, that lender will subsidize the remaining 10 percent owner portion of the finance package.

Generally, the term on a 504 CDC loan is either 10 or 20 years.

International trade.   The SBA Office of International Trade provides a variety of programs geared at encouraging entrepreneurs to enter the global marketplace. One of the office's principal missions is to dispel the notion that international trade is too difficult and expensive for small businesses.

The SBA offers education, outreach, and financing programs to assist small firms to initiate or expand export markets. Services of particular note include:

- An initial consultation with an international trade attorney.
- Matchmaker trade missions, which arrange one-to-one contacts for U.S. firms with trading partners in international markets.
- Nationally and internationally sponsored trade fairs.
- One-on-one counseling with Service Corps of Retired Executives (SCORE) international trade veterans.
- Access to the Export Information System, which provides a glimpse of potential global markets for your product or service.
- Publications and resource guides addressing international trade issues.

For further information on international trade assistance, contact the trade specialist at your local or regional SBA office.

Export Revolving Line of Credit Program (ERLC).   Small firms that have been in business at least one year can qualify for financing under the ERLC. Manufacturers can use fund proceeds to pay for labor and materials for manufacturing goods. Financing under this program can be used to develop foreign markets or to purchase goods and services for export, as well.

Unlimited withdrawals and repayments during a predetermined time frame are allowed through ERLC short-term credit account. The SBA can guarantee 85 percent of loans up to $750,000.

This loan program provides an excellent vehicle for small companies interested in entering the global marketplace.

Small Business Innovation Research Grants (SBIRs). This program gives small technology firms an opportunity to participate in over $500 million in federal government research and development projects. This program supports U.S. technology advancements. Grant awards strengthen small firms and give them an opportunity to explore future product commercialization.

Contracts are awarded through various government agencies, such as the Department of Defense. Solicitations for grants are mailed to interested small firms.

Generally, an announcement for awards proposes a problem. In the first phase, firms are invited to offer a solution. Following phases fund design and testing appropriate products, then production.

The following information gives you a quick loan recap:

Does the SBA have business grants? No, the SBA does not provide grants for the purpose of business start-up or expansion. Information about SBA loans is contained in the information packet available at any district office.

Does my business qualify for SBA assistance? Approximately 98 percent of all businesses are eligible for SBA assistance. Ineligible businesses include those engaged in speculation, lending, or investing and businesses involved in the creation or distribution of ideas, such as newspapers, magazines, and academic schools.

What do I need to do to get an SBA guaranty loan? Research your business idea, and develop a business plan and realistic financial projections and estimates of anticipated earnings. Read the information provided by the SBA, and approach your bank or an SBA lender. Remember, a well-planned and organized presentation will be an important factor in the review of your loan request.

Do I have to be declined by a bank? No, to qualify for a guaranteed loan, you do not have to be turned down by a lender.

What are the loan limits? The SBA does not set loan minimums. The maximum amount that SBA will guarantee is $750,000. Under the long-term export loan program, a maximum of $1,250,000 can be guaranteed. Many lenders will not participate in loans less than $50,000. Yet there are banks that will make loans as low as $25,000.

How much money do I need to have in order to qualify for an SBA loan? The borrower's capital contribution generally must be 25 to 30 percent of the total project cost for business loans.

How long will it take to get my loan? A credit decision on a compete loan package is usually made within 10 working days after it is received by the SBA. This assumes that the borrower and lender have provided all the necessary information.

Where can I get the loan application? SBA loan forms are available from your participating lender. Documentation requirements are stated in the SBA information packet.

Source: Reprinted from: "Small Business Start-up Information Package—Colorado District Office," SBA/SCORE, 1994.

SBA TECHNICAL ASSISTANCE PROGRAMS

Office of Business Development

The Small Business Administration's Office of Business Development offers a variety of programs to assist small businesses. Programs range from individual counseling with entrepreneurs, workshops, courses, and conferences to an array of publications and video tapes.

Whether you are starting a business, looking to expand, or considering international trade, SBA personnel and literature can help you. Business topics include, but are not limited to, marketing, planning, finance, management, expansion, and diversification. Special needs, such as rural business development, global trade, and young business owners, are also addressed.

Some workshops and programs are presented directly by the agency. Others are held in cooperation with local chambers of commerce, colleges, and universities, as well as with independent trade associations. The SBA district office nearest you offers a complete listing of all activities available in any calendar month. Many events are listed in the daily papers and business journals, also.

SBA on-line.   You may contact the SBA by computer modem for a complete listing of programs, services, regulations, contract opportunities, and other information. With your computer baud modem, dial 1-800-859-INFO (for 2400 modems) or 1-800-697-INFO (for 9600 modems).

Service Corps of Retired Executives (SCORE). In over 750 locations throughout the United States, over 13,000 individuals offer help to small businesses via the SCORE program. These volunteers do one-on-one counseling with entrepreneurs on any small-firm problem area, including, but not limited to, employee policies, general operations, cash flow analysis, government regulations, and so forth. Those interested in starting a new business are helped, as well.

SCORE counseling is completely confidential. It is a *free* service. For information on SCORE assistance, contact your local SCORE chapter listed in the federal government section of your local telephone book.

Small Business Institute (SBI). SBIs are organized on over 500 college and university campuses throughout the country. In this program, faculty supervisors guide teams of senior- and graduate-level business-management students as they assist small firms. Students make on-site visits to the business and offer individual counseling, particularly in the areas of planning, accounting, and marketing. Students may also assist local communities on economic development issues.

Counseling to the entrepreneur is *free* of charge. Students receive academic credit for their assistance. Contact your local SBA district office for the SBI program nearest you. (Keep in mind that SBI students are also an excellent resource for new personnel. As the business owner working with the student through the program, you will have the opportunity to assess his or her potential as a future employee.)

Small Business Development Centers (SBDCs). SBDCs provide one-on-one counseling, research studies, technical assistance, and managerial workshops for small business owners. Most often, the SBDC program is managed by a community college, university, chamber of commerce, or state economic development agency and works on a contract basis with the SBA.

Most often, the training provided by the SBDC is curriculum-based and offers practical solutions for small business situations. Both new and growing businesses can benefit from working with an SBDC.

Some workshops are free, while other ongoing course work is fee-based. Some SBDC classes qualify for academic credit.

There are approximately 50 lead SBDC centers and over 600 service facilities throughout the United States. For specific information about SBDC programs, refer to your local telephone directory, state economic development agency, or the SBA office nearest you. Note: Many SBDCs offer strong curriculum studies on international trade issues.

SBDC listings.   For the address and phone number of the Small Business Development Center nearest you, contact your local SBA district office. There are over 60 dstrict offices throughout the United States. In addition there are 10 regional offices. Those offices are listed here for your convenience.

SBA
155 Federal Street
Boston, MA 02110
617-451-2023

SBA
1375 Peach Tree Street NE
Atlanta, GA 30367
404-347-2797

SBA
26 Federal Plaza
Suite 31-08
New York, NY 10278
212-264-1450

SBA
300 South Riverside Drive
Suite 1975 S
Chicago, IL 60606
312-353-5000

SBA
475 Allendale Road
Suite 201
King of Prussia, PA 19406
215-962-3700

SBA
8625 King George Drive
Building C
Dallas, TX 75235
214-767-7633

SBA
911 Walnut Street
Kansas City, MO 64106
816-426-3608

SBA
633 17th Street
7th Floor
Denver, CO 80202
303-294-7186

SBA
71 Stevenson Street
20th Floor
San Francisco, CA 94105
415-744-6402

SBA
2601 Fourth Avenue
Suite 440
Seattle, WA 98121
206-553-5676

Chapter Six

State Programs

In addition to federal small business programs, state governments offer assistance, too. Before contacting them about your company needs, there are a few things you should know.

BUSINESS RETENTION/GROWTH

Today, most state small business programs are based on certain economic assumptions.

1. Retaining and supporting existing businesses saves money. When businesses fail, jobs are lost, production ceases, and downtime is costly.
2. Assisting small firms improves the overall state economy.

Goods/services are produced and sold.

Small business owners are self-sufficient.

Business growth increases job and training opportunities for others.

As a knowledgeable, successful entrepreneur, you are contributing to your state's economic well-being. When you are struggling with a business problem, aid is available. Reaching out for help is in your best interest. What's more, your state government wants you to succeed and benefits from assisting you.

TIMING IS EVERYTHING

When problems occur in a large company, there are committees, financial resources, and time to work them out. Small firms don't have that luxury.

As the adage goes, most small business owners wear all the hats. Unfortunately, that often means that problems go unattended in one area while you put out fires in another. Remember, timing is critical. It's hard for an outsider to help when your predicament reaches an emergency level.

Since your business is your livelihood, you need to envision the future. If issues are on the horizon that are beyond your scope of expertise, get help now.

START-UPS/EMERGING BUSINESSES

State-sponsored programs are excellent for new and growing firms. While states frequently conduct direct small business programs, cooperation with others is key. Typically, states participate in projects with the federal government, community colleges, chambers, local governments, and business-oriented nonprofit organizations.

These combined resources have a double advantage. They help you build your business network quickly while you learn new skills.

SBDCs

All states participate in the federal Small Business Development Center (SBDC) programs. Most centers offer advice, counseling, technical assistance, and resource guidance in many fields. Some offer financing and international trade training. Keep in mind that there are over 600 SBDCs located throughout the United States.

Community Colleges

Many community colleges house SBDCs. Those that do not often offer entrepreneurship classes at nominal costs.

Chambers

Local chambers of commerce can also host small business training programs. Most target programs to suit chamber member needs. For example, a chamber located in a technology-based community may offer more assistance programs around research and development issues.

Business-Oriented Nonprofits

Generally, these organizations have a specific mission. Some are local economic development agencies; others may be funding, technology, or farming cooperatives. Most work with state governments to enhance small business opportunities within their geographic or industry bounds.

WHAT TO EXPECT

State government small business programs vary according to state laws and budget. However, most states offer at least basic assistance in the following areas:

• *Permits and licensing.* Many states provide an information telephone number, usually a small business hot line, to guide you through required business paperwork. This phone service often includes a referral service for other helpful state phone listings.

• *Business development.* This department provides direct or indirect technical assistance, generally through SBDCs or chambers, for start-ups and existing businesses.

• *Ombudsman.* The ombudsman agency helps small businesses with regulatory issues. In some states, it is known as the *Advocacy Office.*

• *Procurement.* This division helps small firms who want to do business with federal, state, or local governments. Some states provide a computer network to:

List upcoming contracts.

Provide government and/or prime contractors with names of small firms.

Cross-reference both.

Other states offer counseling to small businesses on obtaining government work.

- *International trade.* Most frequently, these direct and indirect programs focus on foreign trade technical assistance and training. However, some states also offer trade-financing packages.
- *Minority and women.* This office usually focuses on overcoming roadblocks for minority and women business ownership. Programs generally offer training and technical assistance, and some offer funding.

In a few states, these programs are now called *Economically and/or socially disadvantaged programs.* This title broadens the spectrum of businesses served.

- *Finance.* This division assists small businesses with funding needs. Some states offer direct and indirect loans; others offer financial counseling and referrals. Keep in mind that some states have laws prohibiting direct lending.
- *Economic development corporations.* These are usually nonprofit corporations that receive funds or guarantees from the state government; a few are state-managed. In some cases, these companies are federally designated SBICs, too. (See Chapter Five, "Federal Government Sources.") Many state financing offices refer small businesses to these economic development companies. (Also see Chapter Eight, "Developing Community Loan Funds.")

State departments of commerce are very valuable resources for small businesses. They provide a myriad of free or low-cost services. You should know that most states also distribute helpful publications, and many provide on-line computer assistance.

PRIMARY STATE PROGRAMS

The following provides primary state small business program listings. The format is repeated for each state:

1. Principal address, phone, and in-state 800 number (as available).
2. Business/technical assistance programs.
3. Advocacy office.
4. Procurement programs.

5. International trade programs.
6. Minority and women programs.
7. Finance programs.
8. Economic development corporations and other programs.*

It's important to understand that this is *not* a complete listing for your state. It is a summary of *basic services* available for small businesses.

Some states have numerous program subcategories. Keep in mind, too, that new projects are added frequently and old ones are phased out. It's a good idea to stay up-to-date. At least once a year, contact your state office for a detailed small business program list.

In addition, you should know that industry-specific programs are accessible to you in most states. For example, agriculture-dominant states generally offer numerous programs for small farm-related businesses. States located on international borders and coastlines often assist small businesses with trade and/or port authority programs.

Remember, too, that information is available from your nearest Small Business Administration office on many state-by-state listing publications. Some pamphlets are written by the SBA and are free. Others, which are privately developed as a public service, are free or nominally priced.

---

*These include small business technical assistance or finance programs not listed in Chapter Seven, "Microenterprise Lending Programs" and Chapter Eight, "Developing Community Loan Funds."

STATE SMALL BUSINESS REFERENCES

ALABAMA

Alabama Development Office

401 Adams Avenue

Montgomery, AL 36130-4106

205-242-0400

Small Business Development Consortium 205-934-7260
Research Division 205-242-0400
Small Business Office of Advocacy 205-242-0400
Small Business Assistance Act Procurement 205-242-7250
Office of Minority Business Enterprise 205-242-0400
Economic Development Administration 205-264-7008
Loans/Capital Formation 205-264-5441

ALASKA

Department of Economic Development

State Office Building, Ninth Floor

333 Willoughby Avenue, P.O. Box 110800

Juneau, AK 99811-0800

907-465-2500

800-478-3474
Division of Business Development 907-465-2017
• Small Business Consulting Center
• Economic Development, Fairbanks Native Association, Inc. 907-452-1648
Industrial Development and Export Authority 907-561-8050
Office of International Trade 907-561-5585
Business Development Minority/Women Opportunities 907-562-0330
                                                    800-478-3474

Division of Economic Development 907-465-2017
Division of Investments 907-465-2510

ARIZONA

Arizona Enterprise Development Corporation

Arizona Department of Commerce

3800 North Central, Suite 1500

Phoenix, AZ 85012

602-280-1341

Business Development 602-731-8720

Business Assistance Center 602-280-1480

Business Retention and Expansion 602-280-1350

Commerce and Economic Development Commission 602-280-1328

Enterprise Development Corporation 602-280-1341

Small Business Financing Programs 602-280-1341

ARKANSAS

Arkansas Industrial Development Commission

One State Capitol Mall

Little Rock, AR 72201

501-682-1121

Advocacy 501-682-7325

Science and Technology Authority 501-324-9006

Established Industries 501-682-7315

Small Business Programs 501-682-5275

Office of State Purchasing 501-324-9312

SBA Procurement Assistance 501-324-5871

Agricultural Export Development Program 501-682-3571

Minority Business Development Programs 501-682-1060

Arkansas Capital Corporation 501-682-9247

Bond Guaranty Program 501-682-1151

Research and Development Tax Credit Program 501-682-7310

CALIFORNIA

Office of Small Business

California Trade and Commerce Agency

801 K Street, Suite 1600

Sacramento, CA 95814

916-324-1295

Office of Small Business 916-324-1295
Small Business Helpline 916-327-4357
Small Business Advocate 916-445-3586
New Product Development Program 916-324-1295
Office of Business Development 916-322-3502
Office of Economic Research 916-324-5853
Office of Export Development 916-590-5965
World Trade Commission 916-324-5511
Office of Small and Minority Businesses 916-322-5060
Small Business Loan Guarantee Program 916-445-3586
California Office of Export Finance 714-562-5519

COLORADO

Office of Business Development

1625 Broadway, Suite 1710

Denver, CO 80202

303-892-3840

800-333-7798
FIRST Customized Training Program 303-892-3840
Small Business Hotline 303-592-7798
                            800-333-7789
Office of Regulatory Reform 303-894-7839
Office of Certification 303-894-2355
International Trade Office 303-892-3840
Minority and Women Business Office 303-892-3840

Colorado Housing and Financing Authority 303-297-2432
State Enterprise Zones 303-892-3840

CONNECTICUT

Office of Small Business Services

365 Brook Street

Rocky Hill, CT 06067-34056

203-258-4200
Connecticut Innovations 203-563-5851
Office of Business Ombudsman 203-258-4200
Procurement Assistance Program 203-258-4200
International Trade Division 203-258-4200
Connecticut Development Authority 203-258-7800

DELAWARE

Delaware Development Office

99 Kings Highway

P.O. Box 1401

Dover, DE 19903

302-739-4271
Business Development
Research
Education and Training
Procurement
World Trade Section 302-577-6262
Small Business Revolving Loan and Credit Enhancement Fund 302-739-4271
Delaware Economic Development Authority 302-739-4271

DISTRICT OF COLUMBIA

Office of Business and Economic Development

717 14th Street, NW

Tenth Floor

Washington, DC 20005

202-727-6600
Business and Permit Center 202-727-7010
Office of International Business 202-727-1576
Department of Human Rights andMinority Business Development 202-785-2886
Economic Development Finance Corporation 202-775-8815
Industrial Revenue Bond Program 202-727-6600
Loan Guarantee Program 202-727-1576

FLORIDA

Bureau of Business Assistance

443 Collins Building

107 W. Gaines Street

Tallahassee, FL 32399-2000

904-488-9357

800-342-0771
Small Business Hotline 800-342-0771
Entrepreneurship Network 904-488-9357
Quick Response 904-922-8647
Business Services Section 904-488-9357
Department of Management—Procurement 904-488-1194
Bureau of International Trade Development 904-487-1399
Minority Purchasing Councils 305-757-9690
Small Business and Minority Advocate 904-487-4698
Finance Section 904-488-9357
Bureau of Economic Analysis 904-487-2971

GEORGIA

Department of Industry, Trade, and Tourism

P.O. Box 1776

Atlanta, GA 30301

404-656-3556

Small Business Revitalization Program 404-656-3872
Procurement Program 404-542-6809
International Trade Division 706-542-6809
Office of Small and Minority Affairs 404-656-1794
Finance Division 404-656-3556
Business and Industrial Loan Program
Capital Network
Regional Revolving Loan Funds
Business Loan Guarantee Fund
Business Development Corporation 404-656-3556

HAWAII

Department of Business, Economic Development, and Tourism

Grosvenor Center, Mauka Tower

737 Bishop Street

Suite 1900

Honolulu, HI 96813

808-586-2591

Small Business Information Service 808-586-2600
Business Action Center 808-586-2545
Pacific Business Center 808-956-6286
Government Marketing Assistance Program 808-586-2600
International Business Center 808-587-2797
Financial Assistance Branch 808-586-2576
Native Hawaiian Revolving Loan Fund 808-586-3777

IDAHO

Department of Commerce

700 West State Street

Boise, ID 83720-2700

208-334-2470
Business Network 208-334-2470
Division of Science and Technology 208-334-2470
Division of International Business 208-334-2470
Disadvantaged Business Emphasis 208-344-2531
Innovation Center 208-523-1026
Business Center for Innovation and Development 208-772-0584

ILLINOIS

Small Business Development Center

620 East Adams Street

Fifth Floor

Springfield, IL 62701

217-524-5856

800-252-2923
Business Hotline 800-252-2923
Self-employment Training Program
Small Business Advocacy Program 312-814-3540
Procurement Assistance Program 217-524-0158
Product and Services Exchange 217-785-6310
Export Assistance Program 312-814-7164
International Trade Centers Program 312-814-7170
Minority and Women Business Enterprise 217-785-4320
Small Business Development Loan Program 217-524-5856
Surety Bond Guarantee Program 312-793-5586
Minority and Women Business Loan Program 217-524-5856

INDIANA

Department of Commerce

One North Capitol Avenue

Suite 700

Indianapolis, IN 46204

317-232-8800

Business Development Division 317-232-8888

Permit Assistance Center 317-232-7304

Office of Business Regulatory Ombudsman 317-232-7304

                                          800-824-2476

Government Assistance and Marketing Group 317-264-2820

International Trade Division 317-232-3527

District Export Council 317-582-2300

Women and Minority Business Assistance Program 317-264-2820

Development Finance Authority 317-233-4332

Statewide Certified Development Corporation 317-469-6166

IOWA

Department of Economic Development

200 East Grand Avenue

Des Moines, IA 50309

515-242-4700

800-532-1216

Small Business Helpline 800-532-1216

Small Business Bureau 515-242-4750

Small Business New Jobs Training Program 515-281-9013

Marketing and Business Expansion Bureau 515-242-4735

Division of Business Development 515-242-4707

Office of Ombudsman 515-281-3592

Procurement Outreach Center 319-898-5665

Targeted Small Business Program 515-242-4721

Economic Development Set-Aside 515-242-4831
Self-Employment Loan Program 515-242-4793
Linked Investments for Tomorrow Program 515-281-3287
Targeted Small Business Financial Assistance Program 515-242-4813
Satisfaction Performance Bond Program 515-242-4721

KANSAS

Department of Commerce

400 SW Eighth Street

Fifth Floor

Topeka, KS 66603-3957

913-296-3480
Division of Existing Industry Development 913-296-5298
Industrial Development Division 913-296-3338
Office of Minority Business 913-296-5298
• Procurement Program
• Minority and Women Program
Trade Development Division 913-296-4027
Development Finance Authority 913-296-6747
Venture Capital, Inc. 913-262-7117
Technology Enterprise Corporation 913-296-5272

KENTUCKY

Cabinet for Economic Development

2300 Capital Plaza Tower

Frankfort, KY 40601

502-564-7140

800-626-2250
Business Information Clearinghouse 502-564-4252
                                        800-626-2250

Small and Minority Business Division 502-564-2064
Office of Business and Technology 502-564-4252
Procurement Assistance Program 502-564-4252
Coal Marketing and Export Council 502-564-2562
Department of Financial Assistance 502-564-4554
Investment Capital Network 502-564-7140
Commonwealth Venture Capital Program 502-564-2924
Commonwealth Small Business Development Co. 502-564-4320

LOUISIANA

Department of Economic Development

P.O. Box 94185

Baton Rouge, LA 70804

504-342-3000
Office of Business Development Services 504-342-5893
Division of Minority and Women Enterprise 504-342-5373
• Procurement Program
• Minority and Women Program
Office of Commerce and Industry 504-342-4320
Economic Development Corporation 504-342-5675

MAINE

Department of Economic and Community Development

State House Station #59

Augusta, ME 04333-0949

800-872-3838 (Business Answers)
Office of Business Development (207) 287-3153
• Business Answers
• One-Step Licensing
• Maine Products Marketing Program
• Business Visitation Program

Finance Authority of Maine (FAME) 207-623-3263
Linked Investment Program 207-623-3263
Maine World Trade Association 207-622-0234

MARYLAND

Department of Economic and Employment Development

Redwood Tower

217 East Redwood Street

Baltimore, MD 21202

410-333-6975
Maryland Business Assistance Center 410-333-6975
Procurement Program 410-333-5094
Maryland Office of International Trade 410-333-8189
Office of Minority Affairs 410-225-1843
Small Business Development Financing Authority 410-333-4270
Investment Financing Group 410-333-3103

Council for Economic and Business Opportunity (CEBO)

800 North Charles Street

Suite 300

Baltimore, MD 21201

410-576-2326

MASSACHUSETTS

Office of Business Development

One Ashburton Place

Room 2101

Boston, MA 02108

617-727-3206
Port Authority Trade Development Unit 617-439-5560

Office of International Trade and Investment 617-367-1830
State Office of Minority and Women 617-727-8692
Industrial Finance Authority 617-451-2477
Business Development Corporation 617-350-8877
Technology Development Corporation 617-723-4920

MICHIGAN

Department of Commerce

P.O. Box 30004

Lansing, MI 48909

517-373-1820
Technical Assistance Center 517-373-9017
Business Ombudsman 517-373-9808
Procurement Assistance Program 517-335-1835
International Trade Authority 517-373-3115
Women Business Owners Services 517-373-8431
Strategic Fund 517-373-7551
• Business and Industrial Development Corporations
• Capital Access Program
• Seed Capital Program
• Industrial Development Revenue Bond Program
Export Direct Investment Program 517-373-6390

MINNESOTA

Small Business Assistance Office

500 Metro Square

121 Seventh Place East

St. Paul, MN 55101-2146

612-282-2103

800-657-3858
Bureau of Small Business 612-282-2103

Bureau of Licenses 612-282-2103
Small Business Procurement Program 612-296-2600
Trade Office 612-297-4222
• Export Outreach and Education Division
• Export Finance Authority
• International Marketing and Investment Division
Office of Business Development and Finance 612-297-1391

MISSISSIPPI

Mississippi Department of Economic and Community Development

P.O. Box 849

Jackson, MS 39205-0849

601-359-3449
Business Incubator 601-352-0957
Existing Business and Industry Assistance Division 601-359-3593
Procurement Assistance Office 601-864-2961
International Trade Office 601-359-6672
Jackson Minority Business Development Center 601-362-2260
Office of Minority Business Enterprise 601-359-3448
Business Finance Corporation 601-359-3552

MISSOURI

Missouri Department of Economic Development

Truman State Office Building

301 West High Street

P.O. Box 1157

Jefferson City, MO 65102

314-751-4962

800-523-1434
Business Development Section 314-751-9045
Business Information Programs 314-751-4982

- Business Assistance Center
- Economic Development Information System
- Product Finder

Procurement Program 314-751-3237

International Business Development Program 314-751-4999

MONTANA

Department of Commerce

1424 Ninth Avenue

Helena, MT 59620

406-444-3494

Economic Development Division 406-444-3814

Economic Information Center 406-444-4393

High Plains Development Authority 406-454-1934

Montana Tradeport Authority 406-256-6875

International Trade Program 406-444-4112

Port of Montana 406-723-4321

Disadvantaged Business and Women Business Procurement Assistance 406-444-6337

Board of Investments Office of Development Finance 406-442-0001

Economic Development Administration 406-449-5074

NEBRASKA

Department of Economic Development

P.O. Box 94666

Centennial Mall South

Lincoln, NE 68509-4666

402-471-3747

One-Stop Business Assistance Center 402-471-3782

Business Development Center 402-595-2381

Entrepreneurship Projects 402-471-4803

Existing Business Assistance Division 402-471-4167

Industrial Training Programs 402-471-3780
Skill Training Employment Division 402-471-3780
Procurement Office 308-535-8213
Office of Minority/Women Ownership 402-221-3604
Investment Finance Authority 402-434-3900
Export Promotion 402-471-4668
Economic Development Corporation 402-475-2795

NEVADA

State Development Corporation

350 South Center Street

Suite 310

Reno, NV 89501

702-323-3625
State Development Corporation 702-323-3625
Office of Small Business 702-323-3625
Procurement Outreach Program 702-687-4325
International Economic Development 702-486-7282
Industrial Revenue Bond Program 702-687-4250
Venture Capital Bond Program 702-687-4250
Commission on Economic Development 702-687-4325

NEW HAMPSHIRE

Department of Resources and Economic Development

Four Park Street

Suite 302

Concord, NH 03301

603-271-2391
Public Information and Permitting Unit 603-271-2975
Business and Industrial Development 603-271-2591
Business Visitation Program 603-271-2591

State Apprenticeship Program 603-271-3176
Procurement Technical Assistance Program 603-271-2591
International Trade Resource Center 603-334-6074
Export Promotion Program 603-271-2591
Port Authority 603-436-8500
Business Finance Authority 603-271-2591
• Industrial Revenue Bonds
• Credit Enhancement Programs
Venture Capital Network, Inc. 617-253-7163
Business Development Corporation 603-623-5500

NEW JERSEY

Department of Commerce and Economic Development
20 West State Street
CN 835
Trenton, NJ 08625
609-292-2444
Office of Technical Assistance 609-292-3860
Office of Business Advocacy 609-292-0700
Contract Services Unit 609-984-9835
Set Aside and Certification Office 609-984-9834
Division of International Trade 609-633-3606
Division for Development for Small Businesses and Women and Minority
Businesses 609-292-3860
Economic Development Authority 609-292-1800
• Commercial Lending 609-292-0187

NEW MEXICO

Economic Development Department
P.O. Box 4187
Santa Fe, NM 87502-4187
505-827-0381

Procurement Assistance Program 505-827-0425
Trade Division 505-827-0307
Minority and Small Business Program 505-827-0425
Governor's Commission on the Status of Women 505-841-4662
Economic Development Division 505-827-0300
Business Development Corporation 505-268-1316

NEW YORK

Department of Economic Development

1515 Broadway

51st Floor

New York, NY 10036

212-827-6150

800-782-8369
Business Assistance Hotline 800-782-8369
Division for Small Business 212-827-6140
Training and Technical Assistance 212-827-6145
Small Business Advocacy Program 212-827-6142
Procurement Assistance Program 518-474-7756
Export Marketing Assistance Services 212-827-6200
Minority and Women's Business Division 212-827-6180
Minority and Women Certification 212-827-6270
Job Development Authority 212-818-1700

NORTH CAROLINA

Small Business and Technology Development Center

4509 Creedmoor Road

Suite 201

Raleigh, NC 27612

919-571-4154

919-733-0641
Program 919-571-4154
⌐965
⌐pment Program 919-571-4154
⌐logy Development Center 919-571-4154

117

⌐ DAKOTA

Department of Economic Development and Finance

1833 East Bismarck Expressway

Bismarck, ND 58504

701-221-5300
Business and Commerce Assistance Center 701-857-3825
Office of Federal Procurement Assistance 701-221-5334
International Trade, Economic Development, and Finance 701-221-5300
Women's Business Development 701-221-5300
Native American Business Development 701-221-5300
Finance and Economic Development 701-221-5300

OHIO

Small Business Development Center

77 South High Street

P.O. Box 1001

Columbus, OH 43266

614-466-2711
One-Stop Business Permit Center 614-466-4232
Procurement Technical Assistance Program 614-466-1876
Minority Procurement Service 614-466-5700
Women's Business Resource Program 614-466-4945
Minority Business Resource Program 614-466-5700
Minority Development Loan Program 614-644-7708

OKLAHOMA

Oklahoma Department of Commerce

6601 Broadway Extension

Building Five

Oklahoma City, OK 73116

405-843-9770
Business Expansion program 405-841-5235
Business Services Program 405-841-5227
Research and Planning 405-841-5170
Main Street Program 405-841-5124
Community Affairs and Development 405-841-5326
International Trade Division 405-841-5217
Tribal Government Assistance 405-841-5250
Minority Business Assistance 405-842-5227
Women-Owned Certification 405-841-5242
Capital Resources Network 405-841-5140
Development Finance Authority 405-848-9761

OREGON

Oregon Economic Development Office

77 Summer Street NE

Salem, OR 97310

503-986-0197
Business Information Center/First-Stop Permit Center 503-986-2222
Marketing Services 503-986-0111
Government Contract Acquisition Program 503-269-0709
Department of Administrative Services 503-378-4642
Small Business International Trade Program 503-274-7482
Office of Minority, Women, and Emerging Small Businesses 503-368-5651
Business Finance Section 503-986-0160

PENNSYLVANIA

Department of Commerce

400 Forum Building

Harrisburg, PA 17120

717-783-8950
Office of Small Business 717-783-8950
Bureau of Small Business and Appalachian Development 717-783-5700
Office of Small Business Advocate 717-783-2525
Procurement Office 717-783-5700
Office of International Trade 717-787-7190
Minority and Women Business Enterprise 717-787-7380
Bureau of Women's Business Development 717-787-3339
Minority Business Development Authority 717-783-1127
Capital Loan Fund 717-783-1768
Machine and Equipment Loan Fund 717-783-5046
Employee Ownership Assistance Program 717-787-7120
Revenue Bond and Mortgage Program 717-783-1108
Economic Development Finance Authority 717-783-1108

RHODE ISLAND

Department of Economic Development

7 Jackson Walkway

Providence, RI 02903

401-277-2601
Business Development Division 401-277-2601
• Federal Procurement Program
• International Trade Coordinator
• Office of Minority Business Assistance
• Small Business Loan Fund
• Financing Programs

SOUTH CAROLINA

Enterprise Development, Incorporated

P.O. Box 1149

Columbia, SC 29202

803-737-0888
Existing Business Services Department 803-737-0400
Center for Applied Technology 803-646-4000
Materials Management Office 803-737-0600
Small and Minority Business Assistance 803-734-0657
Southeast Capital Connection 803-737-0888
Jobs Economic Development Authority 803-737-0079

SOUTH DAKOTA

Governor's Office of Economic Development

711 East Wells Avenue

Pierre, SD 57501-3369

605-773-5032
Business Research Bureau 605-677-5287
Procurement Technical Assistance Center 605-677-5498
Export, Trade, and Marketing Division 605-773-5032
Economic Development and Finance Authority 605-773-5032
• Future Fund
• Financial Packaging
• Revolving Economic Development and Initiative Fund

TENNESSEE

Department of Economic and Community Development

320 Sixth Avenue North

Nashville, TN 37243

800-872-7201

Small Business Office 615-741-2626
Small Business Purchasing and Contracts 615-741-7159
Export Office 615-741-5870
Office of Minority Business Enterprise 615-741-2545
Women Business Owners 615-741-2545

TEXAS

Texas Department of Commerce

816 Congress Avenue

P.O. Box 12728

Austin, TX 78711

512-472-5059

800-888-0581
Small Business and Community Economic Development 512-320-9521
Information and Research 800-888-0581
Advanced Technology Marketplace 512-320-9561
International Trade Division 512-320-9637
Small and Minority Business Program 512-463-3419
Business Finance Division 512-320-9634
Capital Development 512-320-9677

UTAH

Community and Economic Development

324 South State Street

Suite 500

Salt Lake City, UT 84111

801-538-8700
Small Business Development 801-581-7905
• Market Information Service
• Innovation Assistance Center
Procurement Outreach Program 801-538-8790

International Business Development 801-538-8737
Office of Asian Affairs 801-538-8883
Office of Black Affairs 801-538-8829
Office of Hispanic Affairs 801-538-8850
Office of Indian Affairs 801-538-8808
Office of Polynesian Affairs 801-538-8691
Capital Access Act 801-538-8776
Technology Finance Corporation 801-364-4346
Economic Development Corporation 801-328-8824

VERMONT

Department of Economic Development
109 State Street
Montpelier, VT 05602
802-828-3221
Small Business Development 802-656-4479
Ombudsman Permit Program 802-828-3221
• Government Procurement Assistance
• International Trade Office
• Minority/Women Contract Procurement Assistance
Economic Development Authority 802-223-7226

VIRGINIA

Office of Small Business and Financial Services
P.O. Box 798
Richmond, VA 23206
804-371-8252
Small Business Development 804-371-8253
Procurement Business Opportunities 804-786-1310
International Trade Division 804-371-0628
Department of Minority Business Enterprise 804-786-5560

Small Business Financing Authority 804-371-8254

Export Financing Program 804-371-8255

WASHINGTON

Business Assistance Center

919 Lakeridge Way SW

Suite A

Olympia, WA 98504-2516

800-237-1233

206-753-5632

Small Business Hotline 800-237-1233

Business Licensing Service 206-753-4401

Small Business Ombudsman 206-586-3022

Business Expansion 206-464-6282

Innovation and Technology Development Assistance 206-464-5450

Office of State Procurement 206-753-0900

Export Assistance Center 206-464-7123

Export Trade Partnership 206-622-2730

Minority and Women Business Enterprises 206-753-9693

Small Business Finance Unit 206-389-2560

Development Loan Fund 206-586-8976

Community Development Finance Program 206-753-2200

Economic Development Authority 206-389-2559

WEST VIRGINIA

Development Office

Capitol Complex

M-145

Charleston, WV 25305

304-558-2234

Small Business Development 304-558-2960
Local Development Initiative 304-558-0121
Business and Industry Finance Development 304-558-2234

WISCONSIN

Department of Development

123 West Washington Avenue

P.O. Box 7970

Madison, WI 53707

800-435-7287

608-266-1018
Permit Information Center 800-976-7894
New or Expanding Business Development 608-266-1018
Small Business Ombudsman 608-266-5489
Bureau of Procurement 608-266-2605
Export Hotline 800-976-7894
Bureau of Minority Development 608-267-9550
• Information Clearinghouse
• Technical Assistance
• Marketing and Certification
Office of Women Business Services 608-266-0593
Start Up and Expansion Loans 608-258-8830
Development Fund 608-264-6151
Export Development Loan Program 608-264-6151
Housing and Economic Development Fund 800-642-6474

WYOMING

Division of Economic and Community Development

Fourth Floor North, Barrett Building

2301 Central Avenue

Cheyenne, WY 82002

307-777-7284

Export Incentive Program 307-777-4457

Science, Technology and Energy Authority 307-766-6797

State Economic Development Loan Program 307-234-5351

Also see Chapter Five, "Federal Government Sources"; Chapter Seven, "Microenterprise Lending Programs"; and Chapter Eight, "Developing Community Loan Funds."

Chapter Seven

Microenterprise Lending Programs

WHY THE FUNDING REVOLUTION

There are revolutionary shifts in small business lending today. The movement is driven by fundamental alterations in the commercial banking industry and a cadre of new small borrowers.

Traditionally, U.S. business-banking relationships helped propel the economy. Capitalism relied on commercial banks' credit extension so small firms could grow.

For generations, small businesses built their companies by borrowing from locally owned, neighborhood banks. In the early years, entrepreneurs were banks' bread-and-butter customers.

Pivotal changes took place in the late 1970s and early 1980s, however, that alter this paradigm. Three significant transformations are worth reviewing.

BANKS

Many large commercial banks were caught up in the boom-and-bust economy. Some of those facilities decided that doing business with big real estate developers provided a greater profit margin with less costs. Gradually, smaller loans were sacrificed. It appeared that economic growth would continue spiraling upward. Risk guidelines were relaxed to accommodate perceived progress, and banks made precarious large loans with less collateral.

When the downturn occurred, some of those banks were unable to substantiate their loan portfolios, and they faltered. Their collapse had a domino effect on the banking industry as a whole.

The tightening economic reality of the late 1980s brought about new, strict regulation. All commercial lenders scrambled to meet requirements, balance their portfolios, and stay profitable.

At approximately the same time, interstate banking laws were initiated. That move prompted strong, healthy banks to buy up smaller banks in other geographical locations. Spectacular improvements in the computer industry also made it convenient for those banks to monitor business transactions from one central locale.

Banks across the nation began merging to survive the economic roller-coaster ride as well as to take advantage of new interstate laws. It's been said that the number of bank holding companies decreased substantially in the 1980s. Projections suggest that bank mergers and buy-outs will continue. This trend negatively impacts small business lending practices.

What these dramatic shifts in commercial lending mean to entrepreneurs is a substantive cut in credit access. Banks are making fewer small loans. While this is an intolerable situation for the national economy, two realities apply.

First, locally owned neighborhood banks are rare today. Most likely, the corner bank is controlled by a national conglomerate, Quick, handshake small loans based on a tradition of good family credit character are the exception rather than the norm.

Second, banks face tough auditing scrutiny, and they know that proper portfolio management takes time and costs money. With that rationale, it is simpler, more cost-effective, and profitable to make one highly collateralized business loan for a million dollars than it is to make 100 small loans totaling a million dollars. This situation might be a solid business decision for banks; however, it adversely affects small businesses by effectively eliminating access to traditional credit for many small borrowers.

SMALL BUSINESSES

The small business dynamic changed, too. There was a time, particularly in the 1950s and 1960s, when it was said that employment with a big corporation meant a "job for life." Jobs with firms such as DuPont, General Electric, Westinghouse, AT&T, and IBM were at a premium.

In the late 1980s, however, most major corporations began tightening their belts and cutting back. Job security became an obscure notion. Corporate restructuring eliminated a plethora of middle-management jobs. The ripple effect terminated many unskilled jobs. National unemployment figures shot up in all categories.

Large numbers of white- and blue-collar employees needed work simultaneously. For many individuals in both groups, small business ownership became a necessary and viable alternative to loss of income. This phenomenon helped create two new small business developments.

Home-Based Businesses

Technological advancements made working from home ideal. Economic constraints made that notion practical. Unemployed mid-level corporate managers reevaluated their skills and applied them to private enterprise. Many entered the service sector as consultants in their fields of expertise.

In the early 1990s, home-based firms began growing at a rapid rate. However, "low overhead" often translated to "no collateral" for small business loans. Home-based businesses increased market share in almost every area, but not in access to capital.

Self-Sufficiency

Unemployed unskilled workers faced new difficulties, too. As computers became mainstream, shifts in corporate employment moved toward technical specialization. Those jobs required different, and often much higher-level, skills. At the same time, competition for unskilled jobs increased.

Fewer jobs, coupled with an excessive labor pool, caused base wages to stagnate. Simultaneously, costs were on the rise. This rapid evolutionary process brought about a significant economic divergence. The gap between the rich and the poor widened pivotally in both urban and rural communities.

Many displaced workers, as well as those individuals trying to help them find employment, came to the same realization: One solution for fewer jobs with big corporations was initiating a very small business venture. Through business ownership, *personal empowerment* and *self-sufficiency* became buzz words of the early 1990s.

MICROENTERPRISE SOLUTIONS

The new small business prototype encourages the growth of very small firms known as microenterprises. By definition, a microenterprise is a sole proprietorship, partnership, or family business with fewer than five employees and initial credit needs under $15,000[1] Both home-based and self-sufficient business ownerships often fit this dynamic.

The grassroots movement toward low-overhead small business ownership helps create a lending/borrowing paradox. While banks are gearing up to write larger loans, a new industry of microentrepeneurs needs to borrow *less* money.

Tightened bank regulation also impacts this credit cycle. To prevent mirroring another banking crisis like the one that occurred in the late 1980s, both federal and state regulators limited commercial bank lending practices. Ironically, there is more money available to lend today. However, fewer small businesses meet the increased collateralization and higher credit standards established by banks to maintain their own asset/lending ratio requirements.

Statistically, small firms are the backbone of the U.S. economy. Small firms generated 68 percent of all new jobs from 1977 to 1987.

In the years 1988 to 1990, small businesses created *all* net new jobs, with the most growth occurring in the firms of fewer than 20 employees.[2]

---

[1]Margaret Clark, Self-Employment Learning Project, *Fact Sheet*, Aspen Institute, 1994.

[2]United States Small Business Administration, *The State of Small Business: A Report of the President*, 1992.

Bank lending should provide a necessary tool to help those businesses expand. The dichotomy created by the widening gap beween banks and small businesses produced a national call for intervention.

In the late 1980s, community groups began using the Community Reinvestment Act (CRA)[3] to pressure banks. In turn, the Federal Reserve used the CRA to halt bank sales or postpone mergers indefinitely if there was evidence that the banks involved in the transaction were not lending appropriately within their respective communities.

While the CRA gave community activist groups and the Federal Reserve a vehicle to push for relevent neighborhood small lending, it did not change the regulations put on banks to tighten credit analysis. This paradox forced nationally chartered commercial banks to seek out new ways to reach small business borrowers.

At the same time, nonprofit organizations, state social service departments, foundations, and microentrepreneurs began talking to one another about self-employment growth. The chief complaint was lack of credit available for small firms.

Finding Models

Across the country, pocket organizations, armed with endowment grants, started experimenting with nontraditional, nonbank lending techniques. Most of these groups built their models on Third World self-sufficiency development programs.

One successful prototype was Accion International. Accion is a nonprofit organization founded in 1961. It makes market-rate microenterprise loans through local affiliate groups in 17 Latin American countries. In 1989, for example, Accion loaned approximately $25 million in amounts that averaged $300 each.

While the amounts are small, that equates to a staggering 83,000 plus loans granted, managed, and collected by one organization

---

[3]The Community Reinvestment Act was passed by Congress in 1975 with relatively little fanfare. However, in 1987, verbiage added to the act gave the Federal Reserve authority to deny bank sales and mergers in instances where banks involved in the transaction did not demonstrate community responsibility.

in a calendar year. Even more important, Accion borrowers sel-
dom had available collateral, yet managed an unparalleled repayment rate of 98 percent.[4]

Accion's success and the growth of other similar programs in
Third World nations, such as Grameen Bank of Bangladesh, sponsored by World Bank, gave hope to those in the United States
seeking a methodology for making small loans workable outside the traditional bank small business lending model.

Getting Organized

In the summer of 1991, 154 individuals from 30 states, representing foundations, 100 experimental lending projects,
practitioners, advocates, and local, state, and federal governments
came together for the first time in Berkeley, California, to discuss
microlending in the United States. That meeting, sponsored by
the Corporation for Enterprise Development, Aspen Institute's
Self-Employment Learning Project (SELP), and the Charles
Stewart Mott Foundation spawned the Association for Enterprise
Opportunity (AEO).[5]

The AEO mission was to provide its membership a forum and
a voice to promote enterprise opportunity for people and communities with limited access to economic resources. With the cooperation of eight foundations and under the direction of its newly
elected national board, AEO became the umbrella microenterprise
organization in the United States.

Interestingly, AEO found that the fledgling experimental lending groups, scattered throughout the country and now joined
under one banner, were as diverse as any random collection of
entrepeneurs.

Some programs followed the Accion Latin America model
closely, lending small amounts of money to groups of microentrepreneurs. Other programs more nearly resembled bank
models, loaning up to $25,000 to individual small firms. That

---

[4]Accion International, *About Accion International*, Agency for International
Development (AID), 1990

[5]*Summary Report: Association for Enterprise Opportunity, Organizing Event*, Association
for Enterprise Opportunity, June 1991.

meant that the United States was creating a wide array of microenterprise lending programs at a rapid pace, with a breadth far surpassing that of the original prototypes in other countries.

Sponsored by a grant from the Charles Stewart Mott and Ford Foundations, the Self-Employment Learning Project set out on a three-year evidentiary data-gathering study to track the growth of the U.S. microenterprise phenomenon. In the meantime, working through its national network, the Association for Enterprise Opportunity member organizations lobbied Congress, state governments, banks, and foundations. Those efforts, coupled with the continued grassroots movement to initiate new model programs, moved venerable mountains.

By 1994, the number of participating lending groups grew to over 200. That's an astounding growth rate for a new lending industry.

SBA Contribution

Under public pressure, government agencies and commercial banks responded quickly to the call for new ways of funding small businesses. The Small Business Administration (SBA) was authorized to begin the Microloan Demonstration Program on October 28, 1991, when the president signed Public Law 102-140, the Commerce, Justice, and State Judiciary, and Related Agencies Appropriations Act of 1992.[6]

Through this project, the Small Business Administration loaned money and made grants to selected private nonprofit organizations. Those groups made matching contributions and, in turn, made microloans and provided technical assistance to eligible small businesses.

In 1992, its first year, the SBA Microloan Program loaned 35 nonprofit programs throughout the country between $250,000 and $750,000 each. Those groups were responsible for loaning those funds out to small firms within their geographical area in amounts not to exceed $25,000 per borrower.

---

[6]United States Small Business Administration, Microloan Demonstration Program, Office of Financial Assistance, Announcement # OFA-92-0001, 1992

In addition to the funds loaned by the SBA, the act authorized a provision for a technical assistance grant to each nonprofit agency lender, or "service provider." That grant amount could not exceed 20 percent of the loan amount in the first two years of participation. The grant portion of the act enabled lenders to assist small firms with such issues as business-plan development, accounting procedures, market analysis, and other specific details essential to making a small business successful.

The SBA Microloan Program is authorized through fiscal year 1995. A total number of 60 nonprofit groups are funded under this authorization. Up to $1,250,000 may be loaned to any one organization over the authorized term. The selected nonprofit groups must repay the SBA within 10 years.

Bank Participation

The advent of the Microloan Program, coupled with the success of other grant/lending programs made available by foundations to nonprofit agencies for model lending projects, spurred many commercial banks to take action. While banks found loaning small amounts of money to individual entrepreneurs difficult, they could make grants and/or loans to nonprofit organizations by following existing archetypes. By doing so, they could also fulfill their CRA obligation to their respective communities.

Through microlending, there was a vehicle available to bring large banks and fledgling small enterprises together again. There are several advantages to both banks and service-provider agencies in bridging this funding chasm through partnerships. Keep in mind that historical small business/banking relationships were often "handshake" deals. Funding microlending programs through grants and loans to nonprofits helps put banks back in the "credit character," or handshake business, without jeopardizing regulatory requirements or forgoing profits.

There's another advantage, too: Banks do make loans comfortably to emerging small firms with a three-year track record, proper accounting documents, proven technical skills, and collateral. Working through service-provider agencies, banks can help "grow" future small business customers.

Nonprofit agencies benefit as well. There is a greater access to capital for their clients and assistance from bank staff on matters of credit analysis. In some situations, banks also offer agency clients no-fee checking accounts and automatic loan repayment transfers.

Service Providers

The American revolution in small business funding puts the burden of success or failure on the emerging service-provider organizations. They are a diversified group, offering a wide assortment of loan packages and entrepreneurial training.

As these groups strive to stay competitive and self-sustainable—a complicated juggling act made more difficult by their fledgling lender status—they give the nation a new way of doing business. Small loans made to microenterprises provide jobs and build the national economy one small business at a time.

As is true with all grassroots movements, there are bound to be minidisasters as well as shining examples of success along the way. But if the middle ground represents a flourishing entrepreneurial monetary resource, then all small business borrowers will ultimately benefit from this new paradigm.

MICROLENDING PROGRAMS

Microenterprise loan pools bring a new dimension to the hands-off commercial lending approach. For the most part, these service-provider organizations are specifically charged with the responsibility of guiding entrepreneurs through virtually every aspect of their business—often *before* and *during* the lending process.

U.S. microenterprise lenders differ from Third World programs in the technical assistance area. For example, Accion Latin America microenterprise models provide no technical assistance.

Accion's programs also require little or no collateral; however, group borrowing techniques create a "peer pressure" dynamic that guides repayment.

In the Accion prototype, money is loaned to a group of five to seven borrowers. Only one or two borrowers get the money; however, all group members are responsible for the loan. Then, too, if any one individual is late on a loan payment, no other group member may borrow until that delinquent loan is brought current.

A training and technical assistance provision in most U.S. microenterprise lending models allows for diversity in the way funds are dispersed. Some funds lend directly to an individual entrepreneur, while others provide group loans only.

Training requirements prior to funding differ as well. For example, there are major dissimilarities in training and technical assistance among the five organizations participating in the Self-Employment Learning Project study. One microloan fund requires 84 hours of workshop participation prior to granting a loan. Another agency, which lends almost entirely to more established firms, has no training requirement.[7]

The wide variety of micrenterprise loan programs available in the United States allows small business owners an opportunity to pick a program that will suit their needs. As of this writing, program growth tends to parallel population size. Microlending projects are on the rise in both urban and rural areas.

RESOURCES

Immediately following this section, you will find a listing of most microlending programs in the United States. The field is new and growing fast. If there is not a program shown in your area, contact any of the national programs for assistance. (National programs follow state listings.) A local program might be in the beginning stages.

You could also contact the nearest SBA office (See Chapter Five, "Federal Government Sources") or your state office of business development. (See Chapter Six, "State Resources.")

---

[7]Margaret Clark, *Self-Employment Leasing Project*, Aspen Institute, 1992.

Keep in mind that starting a community lending fund in your area is a viable alternative. Your firm and other small businesses in your community will reap the benefits. (See Chapter Eight, "Developing Community Loan Funds.")

MICROENTERPRISE LOAN PROGRAMS

The following index is a by-state guide to organizations that support microenterprise principles. Some groups provide advice and technical assistance; most make direct loans.

ALASKA

Interior Alaska Economic Development Council (IAEDC)
New Routes
520 5th Avenue, Suite 410
Fairbanks, AK 99701
(907) 459-1310
FAX (907) 456-1942
Contact: Cynthia Marquette

This organization was founded in January 1989 to promote a sound community, self-sufficiency, employment, business, and industrial opportunities through balanced, diversified, stable, long-term growth, with maximum development of human and natural resources. The mission is to develop an opportunity for all the people of interior Alaska to build a confident community that emphasizes cooperation and coordination of action, anticipation of human needs, and encouragement for meeting these needs. IAEDC is open to all Alaskans.

Technical assistance includes development of grant and loan applications, business training courses, individual business counseling, peer support programs, and research on financial assistance.

Nonbusiness support services include individual counseling for artists and nonprofits, funding research, development of grant proposals, grants writing classes, and workshops.

Achievements show that after 27 months of operation, the New Routes program has an average of 75 percent success rate by proposal/loan.

Future plans include disseminating the New Routes program throughout Alaska.

The annual operating budget is $300,000. Sources of funding include local and state funding, private foundations, corporate grants, and user fees.

Note: Information as of 1992

ARIZONA

National Center for American Indian Enterprise Development
953 East Juanita Avenue
Mesa, AZ 85204
(602) 831-2331
(800) 423-0452
FAX (602) 491-1332
Contact: Steven Stalling

Northwest Region
19033 West Valley Highway, Suite D-101
Kent, WA 98032
(206) 656-8401
FAX (206) 656-8411
Contact: Crystal Pierce, VP

Pacific Region
9650 Flair Drive, Suite 303
El Monte, CA 91731
(818) 442-3701
FAX (818) 442-7115
Contact: Francisco Jiminez, VP

Southwest Region
953 East Juanita Avenue
Mesa, AZ 85204
(602) 831-7524
FAX (602) 491-1332
Contact: Kenneth Robbins, VP

This agency was founded in 1970 to develop and expand an American Indian private sector that employs Indian labor, increases the number of viable Indian businesses, and positively impacts and involves reservation communities by establishing business relationships between tribal enterprises and private industry.

The target population is tribal enterprises and privately owned Indian enterprises on a national basis.

Technical assistance includes business training courses, individual business counseling, peer support and exchange, and Commerce Business Daily On-Line.

Achievements show more than 1,000 tribal and Indian-owned businesses started or expanded; these ventures have a success rate of 95 percent. The National Center delivered over 300 training sessions with over 3,500 participants completing these sessions. The $215 million in financing and contracts secured for clients demonstrates the National Center's effectiveness.

Ideas for the future are reservation business market opportunity research, SBA assistance, SBA regional tribal forums, manufacturers' representatives services, and national Indian trade organizations.

The annual operating budget is approximately $1 million. Sources of funding are contracts and grants from government agencies, corporations, and philanthropic groups.

Note: Information as of 1992

Micro Industry Credit Rural Organization (MICRO)
802 East 46th Street
Tucson, AZ 85713
(602) 622-3553
(602) 622-1480
Contact: Frank Ballesteros

This organization was founded in August 1986 to stabilize and encourage the growth of microenterprises in the southwestern United States through credit and technical assistance and organizing microassociations.

Geographic areas include Cochise, Yuma, Santa Cruz, Pima, and Maricopa counties in Arizona and Imperial county in California. Emphasis is on female and Hispanic populations in border areas of southern Arizona and California.

Technical assistance includes business training courses, basic bookkeeping, tax seminars, individual business counseling, peer support and exchange, business expositions, mentoring, a large business-to-small business adopt-a-business program, and associations in each community.

Financing is given to individual borrowers. Loans range in size from $500 to $10,000. The average loan is $1,618. Loan terms range from 6 months to 24 months, with an average of 9 months.

Nonsupport services include individual mental health counseling. Other elements of the program include savings, an emergency loan fund for members, technical assistance, marketing for international markets, and an association of microenterprise development in each target area.

Achievements show that in five years MICRO dispersed over $1 million to over 350 microbusinesses, stabilized over 200 businesses, and created over 400 jobs in the rural areas of southern Arizona and California.

In 1989, MICRO was the recipient of the first Charles T. Grigsby Award for its innovative economic development project.

Future plans include strengthening each microbusiness association to the point of having it become a nonprofit corporation. MICRO will then issue a major line of credit to the associations. The associations will, in turn, loan out to their association members. MICRO plans to be an Arizona statewide program offering its services in nine counties.

The annual operating budget is $443,000, and the loan capital fund is $1,000,000.

Sources of funding include Ford Foundation PRI, the Arizona Department of Commerce, Sisters of Charity, Hitachi, C.S. Mott Foundation, and TIDES Foundation.

Note: Information as of 1992.

ARKANSAS

Good Faith Fund
1210 Cherry Street, Suite 9
Pine Bluff, AR 71601
(501) 535-6233
FAX (501) 535-0741
Contact: Julia Vindasius

This organization was begun in May 1988 as an umbrella organization to Southern Development Bancorporation to widen the profile of future entrepreneurs to include women, minorities, and dislocated workers through the delivery of credit and credit services and to raise income levels of low-income, self-employed individuals.

The target population is low- and moderate-income people, women, and minorities in seven counties in Southeast Arkansas.

Technical assistance includes peer support, networking and exchange, meetings and workshops, borrowing group orientation and training, a group savings program, and ad hoc technical assistance.

Financing is provided for group lending. The number of groups formed is nine, and loan sizes range up to $5,000; the first-time limit is up to $1,200. The loan size average is $1,200, and loan terms range from 3 to 18 months, with the average being one year.

Market rate determines the interest charged. Per Arkansas usury law, commercial rate is limited to five points above the discount rate.

Other elements of the program are savings, technical assistance, and special action research initiatives for productive sectors such as day care, crafts, and so forth.

Achievements include development of welfare demonstration project, and recruitment and the hiring of new field staff.

Future plans include managing and expanding loan volume and quality membership, exploring sectoral intervention/networks as a way to reach more people efficiently, and pursuing programs to ensure that self-employment is a choice or option for welfare recipients who aim to be self-sufficient.

The annual budget is $475,000, and the loan capital fund is $500,000.

Sources of funding include Winthrop Rockefeller Foundation, Levi Strauss Foundation, Ford Foundation, C.S. Mott Foundation, Ms. Collaborative for Women's Economic Development, and other private foundations.

Note: Information as of 1992.

CALIFORNIA

American Woman's Economic Development Corp.
Starting Your Own Business
Managing Your Own Business
Global Marketing
230 Pine Avenue, Third Floor
Long Beach, CA 90802
(310) 983-3747
FAX: (310) 983-3750
Contact: Judith Luther, executive director

This agency was established in December 1990 as an umbrella group of AWED/New York. It has since become an independent affiliate. The goals are to provide long-term, affordable training to female business owners or women who wish to go into business. The target population includes low-income, multicultural, and multiprofessional women.

Technical assistance provided includes business training courses, individual business counseling, peer support and exchange, and mentoring.

The agency raised $60,000 of scholarship money for low-income women in the first six months; marketed to non-English speaking communities; and enrolled Latino, Cambodian, Chinese, Japanese, Korean, Native American, and African-American women, as well as non-Hispanic white women.

The future plans include development of a corps of multilingual trainers who can train effectively in Los Angeles's diverse communities as well as in Mexico, Japan, and so forth.

AWED's annual operating budget is $700,000.

Coalition for Women's Economic Development (CWED)
Micro-Business Workshop
Solidarity Circle
Revolving Loan Fund
315 West Ninth Street, Suite 705
Los Angeles, CA 90015

(213) 489-4995
FAX: (213) 489-4090
Contact Person: Gail Carter

CWED served over 400 women, including workshop graduates and Circle members. CWED has provided information to local, state, and national officials regarding microenterprise development. CWED, which is a member of the Los Angeles City Council's Street Vendors Task Force, held the first annual Women's Luncheon in May 1991, which was very successful.

CWED plans to administer its programs throughout southern California by 1995. CWED also hopes to establish permanent community workshop centers to assist local residents in achieving skills for successful self-employment.

Technical assistance provided includes business training courses, individual business counseling, peer support and exchange, and mentoring. CWED Network Association graduates of workshops and Solidarity Circle members are eligible to join.

Financing is for individual borrowers. Loan sizes range from $50 to $2,000. The loan size average is $2,000, and the loan term average is one year. For group borrowers, the loan size range is $50 to $2,000, with an average of $1,700, and the loan term range is one year.

Community Ventures, Inc.
Child Care Revolving Loan Program
512 Front Street
Santa Cruz, CA 95060
Formal Affiliation: Santa Cruz Community Credit Union (SCCCU)
(408) 425-4824
FAX (408) 425-4824
Contact: Jeff Wells, president

This agency was founded in September 1990 to provide technical and financial assistance to businesses that cannot be served by the Community Credit Union due to regulatory constraints.

The geographic area is Santa Cruz County. The target market is female- and minority-owned businesses and low-income people.

Technical assistance includes business training courses, workshops, and individual business counseling with loan officers.

Financing is offered to individual borrowers. Loan sizes range from $1,500 to $15,000, and average $5,000. Loan terms range from one to five years, with an average of two years.

Community Ventures, Inc., achievements include making loans to nonprofit organizations through the Child Care Revolving Loan Program, which established child care for over 150 children.

The annual operating budget is $10,000. The loan capital fund is $310,000. Sources of funding include SCCCU, foundations, grants, and the county of Santa Cruz.

North Coast Opportunities
Bright Center Rural Economic Development Project
413 North State
Ukiah, CA 95482
(707) 462-8945
FAX (707) 462-8945
Contact: Patty Steinburg

This agency provides training and services that enable microenterprises to be created and expanded to bring additional capital into the community, to create new jobs, and to assist low-income people to achieve and maintain economic self-sufficiency.

The geographic area is limited to Mendocino County, California. It serves people in this county with an emphasis on low-income people.

Technical assistance provided includes business training, individual business counseling, peer support and exchange, mentoring, and marketing lab. Financing is administered by a partner agency, the WEST Company.

Nonbusiness support services include individual counseling, child care, and transportation. Other elements of this program include a savings program.

Achievements include integrated personal development with business development training and the development of a successful women's program.

The annual operating budget is $210,000. The loan capital fund is administered by The WEST Company.

Note: Information as of 1992.

North Coast Small Business Development Center
882 H Street
Crescent City, CA 95531
(707) 464-2168
Contact: Frances Clark

This agency, started in 1987, is part of the California SBA Small Business Development Center network.

Its geographic area includes Humbolt and Del Norte counties of California. The program targets small businesses in the local rural area.

Technical assistance includes business training courses and individual business counseling.

Future plans include obtaining certification for bidding on state contracts and then pursuing development of a microenterprise loan program, targeting cottage industries, and Indian industry.

The annual operating budget is $100,000.

Note: Information as of 1992.

San Francisco Mayor's Office of Community Development
Self-Employment and Economic Development Program (SEED)
10 United Nations Plaza, Suite 600
San Francisco, CA 94102
(415) 554-8765
FAX (415) 554-8769
Contact: Jay Smith

This organization, begun in 1985,. is an umbrella group for the San Francisco Mayor's Office. Its mission is determined by Title 1 of the Housing and Community Development Act of 1974, whose primary objective is the development of viable urban communities. The Mayor's Office of Community Development is the city agency with the responsibility of fostering an improved standard of living for San Francisco's low- and moderate-income residents.

The geographic area is limited to San Francisco, targeting low- and moderate-income San Franciscans, with a focus on minority and women entrepreneurs.

Technical assistance includes business training courses, individual business counseling, peer support and exchange, mentoring, and prebusiness training.

Financing is given to individual borrowers. Loan sizes range from $1,000 to $15,000, with an average loan size of $5,000. Loan terms average two years.

Achievements include over 200 businesses started or expanded, and over 300 secondary jobs created by these businesses. Future plans are to formalize extended outreach to public housing residents.

SEED's annual budget is $18 million, and the loan capital fund is $100,000.

Note: Information as of 1992.

San Francisco Renaissance (SFR)
Micro Business Incubator
1453 Mission Street, Sixth Floor
San Francisco, CA 94103
(415) 863-5337
FAX (415) 863-5471

This organization was started in 1985 to increase self-employment and business ownership among low-income people and minorities to bring jobs and capital to the urban community.

The geographic area includes San Francisco and the surrounding Bay area. Target markets are low-income people, women, and minorities.

Technical assistance provided includes business training courses, individual business counseling, peer support and exchange, and mentoring.

Nonbusiness support services include individual counseling.

SFR launched the first microbusiness incubator in San Francisco in 1989. The purpose of the business incubator is to reduce the cost of operating overhead and provide a nurturing environment for start-up businesses. An additional support service includes an"incubator without walls" business assistance center. This service gives graduates access to business support services without the full cost of renting an actual office.

Future plans include development of a consulting component to transfer technology and expertise to other groups, expansion of the incubator and business assistance center, and development of innovative methods for reaching residents of public housing.

SFR's annual budget is $275,000. Funding sources are local government, foundations, tuition, and fees.

Note: Information as of 1992.

Santa Cruz Community Credit Union
Community Development Loan Program
512 Front Street
Santa Cruz, CA 95060
(408) 425-7708
FAX: (408) 425-4824

This organization was founded in 1977 to provide technical and financial assistance for small businesses, with particular emphasis on female-, minority-, and worker-owned businesses, cooperatives, and nonprofits; to provide assistance to businesses that enhance the environment or serve the low-income community; and to assist businesses promoting affordable housing or democracy in the workplace.

The target population includes low-income people, women, and minorities in Santa Cruz County.

Technical assistance includes business training courses, individual business counseling, and peer support and exchange.

Financing is available to individual borrowers. Loan sizes range from $1,500 to $250,000, with a loan average of $15,000. Loan terms range from two months to seven years, with an average term of two years. The number of loans to date is over 1,000, with a dollar value of over $24 million.

SCCCU is one of the largest community development credit unions in the United States, with $2.4 million loaned to women- and minority-owned businesses, $3 million in loans to farmers and farming co-ops practicing organic or integrated pest-management techniques, over $1 million in loans to affordable housing projects, $786,000 in earthquake disaster loans, and over $1 million in loans to nonprofits.

The annual operating budget is $1.4 million, and the loan capital fund is $19 million.

Note: Information as of 1992.

WEST Company
Women's Economic Self-Sufficiency Training
413 North State Street
Ukiah, CA 95482
(707) 462-2348
Contact: Sheilah Rogers

This organization was started in November 1988 for the purpose of stimulating and catalyzing the development of new economic opportunities for people in Mendocino County, with particular emphasis on creating jobs and facilitating the development of skills that expand the economic options of low-income people.

The target population is low-income people in Mendocino County in northern California.

Technical assistance includes business development training, individual business counseling, peer support and exchange, mentoring, marketing lab in development, business seminars, and conferences.

Financing is provided for individual borrowers. Loan sizes range from $100 to $5,000. Group borrowers' loan sizes range from $550 to $1,500; the average is $750. The loan term is one year.

The WEST Company's annual operating budget is $202,000, and the loan capital fund is $38,000.

Funding sources include James Irving Foundation, the U.S. SBA/Office of Women's Business Ownership, and the Community Services Discretionary Grant.

Note: Information as of 1992.

Women Entrepreneurs
Self-Employment Training Opportunities
445 West Weber, Suite 140
Stockton, CA 95203
(204) 467-4803
Contact: Kristal Yee

This organization was founded in 1991 to provide education, technical training, and financial assistance to empower low-income women to achieve their goal to become self-sufficient.

The target population is low-income women (determined by U.S. Housing and Urban Development guidelines) and women on welfare and other public assistance in San Jocquin County, California.

Technical assistance includes business training courses, individual business counseling, peer support and exchange, and mentoring.

Financing is given to individual borrowers. Loan sizes range from $100 to $3,000.

Future plans include increasing geographic coverage, achieving a stronger community commitment to the program, promoting women in business, exploring new ways of assisting women to achieve economic independence, and working with traditional lending sources to increase opportunities for low-income women in business.

Women Entrepreneurs' annual operating budget is $120,000. Funding sources are the City of Stockton, private contributions, and foundations.

Note: Information as of 1992.

Women's Business Network
551 Valle Vista
Oakland, CA 94610
(415) 271-0165
Contact: Jelen Lupowizt

This organization was begun in July 1990 as an umbrella group of Women's Building of San Francisco. Its purpose is to provide practical peer support to women in business through business events, expos, and workshops in order to help women achieve economic independence through self-employment.

The target population is women in the first five years of their businesses in Alameda County and San Francisco.

Technical assistance includes peer support and exchange, mentoring, and bi-monthly events.

Agency achievements include having over 700 women attend seven events and having 100 members join in 10 months.

Future plans include instituting a low-interest loan fund and a technical support program, finding new chapters in the Bay area and California, and making an educational documentary.

Note: Information as of 1992.

Women's Economic Growth
P.O. Box 391
325 Miner Street
Yreka, CA 96097
(916) 842-1571
or
P.O. Box 605
423 Main Street
Etna, CA 96027
(916) 467-3100
Contact: Mimi Van Sickle

This organization was founded in 1988 to promote the economic self-sufficiency of women in Siskiyou County through innovative business development services.

The target population is low-income individuals and women in Siskiyou County.

Technical assistance includes business training courses, individual business counseling, peer support, and mentoring.

Financing is for individual and group borrowers. Loan sizes range up to $10,000 for individuals, and loan terms vary according to borrower. The interest rate is below market rate. For group borrowers, the loan size range is up to $5,000.

Nonbusiness support services include: child care, full reimbursement to business training participants, transportation, and mileage reimbursement to business training participants.

WEG's annual operating budget is $250,000. The loan capital fund is $111,000. Funding sources are federal and state governments, foundations, and private donations.

Note: Information as of 1992.

Women's Initiative for Self-Employment (WISE)
P.O. Box 192145
San Francisco, CA 94119-2145
(415) 624-3351
FAX (415) 512-9471

This organization was established in October 1988 to link lower-income women with skills, information, and financing necessary for small business success. It works to remove institutional barriers preventing women's equal participation in our economy.

The target population includes low- and moderate-income women. The loan fund is limited to those in San Francisco and Alameda counties only. All other program components are available throughout the greater Bay Area.

Technical assistance includes business training courses, individual business consulting, sector-based support groups, mentoring, postlending management assistance, Spanish-language business training services, and a homeless women's business training pilot.

Financing is for individual borrowers. Loan sizes range up to $10,000 and the loan average is $4,500 to $5,000. Loan terms range from 7 to 36 months, and the term average is 25 months.

Nonbusiness support services include available child care stipends and available transportation stipends on a limited basis.

WISE's annual operating budget is $493,034. The loan capital fund is $253,225. Sources of funding are foundations, corporations, banks, Community Development Block Grants (CDBG), and individual support.

Note: Information as of 1992.

COLORADO

Greater Denver Local Development Fund (GDLDC)

P.O. Box 2135
Denver, CO 80201-2135
(303) 296-9535

This organization was established in 1976 for the purpose of community and economic development. GDLDC's mission is to provide business loans and technical assistance to entrepreneurs who cannot obtain traditional financing, enabling them to achieve self-sufficiency and have a positive impact on their community.

The target population is businesses based in Adams, Arapahoe, Boulder, Denver, or Jefferson Counties.

GDLDC has an intensive technical assistance program, which is focused primarily on borrowers. It provides individualized consulting, with special emphasis on marketing and cash flow management. The organization also arranges mentor relationships, conducts training workshops, facilitates networking with other borrowers, and is developing a resource pool of volunteers from the business community.

Financing is for individual borrowers, either start-ups or expanding businesses, with some potential for being bankable in the future. The maximum loan amount is $25,000. The average loan amount is $14,000. Interest rates and fees vary with market rates.

Funding sources include private foundations, corporations, banks and the U.S. Small Business Administration. The loan capital fund is $850,000.

Mi Casa Resource Center for Women

The Business Center for Women
571 Galapago Street
Denver, CO 80204
(303) 572-1302
FAX (303) 595-0422

This agency was founded in 1977, and the program began in 1991 to assist women in developing and starting new businesses or in developing and expanding existing businesses. The program goal is to help women develop the skills to be successful business owners.

The target population is low-income women in the state of Colorado.

Technical assistance includes business training courses, individual business counseling in English and Spanish, peer support and exchange, mentoring, and special monthly seminar topics.

Financing is for group borrowers. Loan sizes range from $500 to $5,000, and the interest rate is prime plus 2 percent.

Nonbusiness support services include referral to other programs at Mi Casa for employment and GED classes.

Future plans include maintaining a very mission-driven organization, offering programs that contribute to women's economic self-sufficiency. The agency hopes to offer the services of the Business Center to welfare recipients in the near future and to run an entrepreneurial program for youth.

The annual budget is $147,000.

Office of Business/Small Business Office
Colorado Leading Edge
1625 Broadway, Suite 1710
Denver, CO 80224
(303) 892-3848

This organization was founded in 1987 to provide statewide management and technical and loan packaging assistance at no cost to new and existing businesses through the Colorado Leading Edge training program, one-on-one consulting, and specific training programs and seminars.

The target population includes small business owners and home-based businesses throughout the state of Colorado.

Technical assistance provided includes business training courses via Colorado Leading Edge, individual business counseling via Small Business Development centers, and peer support and exchange for women and minority businesses.

Financing is for group borrowers. Loan sizes range up to $25,000, and the loan term is up to three years.

Achievements include founding 18 Small Business Development centers statewide. The Small Business Hot Line ([800] 333-7798 and [800] 592-5920) assists 2,000 new and expanding businesses a month by providing information on licenses, permits, and management assistance.

Colorado Leading Edge is a small business training program that offers 60 hours of intensive training, help in preparing a business plan, and one-on-one counseling sessions.

Future plans include working on providing loans through banks to businesses that have gone through training and have a business plan in hand. Leading Edge also offers finance training for women business owners.

The annual operating budget for the Leading Edge Program is $130,000.

Note: Information as of 1992.

CONNECTICUT

Greater Hartford Business Development Center, Inc. (GHBDC)
15 Lewis Street, Room 204
Hartford, CT 06103
(201) 527-1301
FAX: (201) 727-9224

This agency was founded in 1976 for the creation and retention of jobs and the creation of tax property.

The target population includes anyone operating or wishing to open a business in Hartford, Connecticut. This business development center's geographic area is limited to Hartford and surrounding towns.

The service that GHBDC provides is financing to individual borrowers. Loan sizes range from $1,450 to $650,000, and the average loan size is $34,300. Loan terms range from 9 to 20 years. The average loan term is seven years.

Achievements include making 235 loans to date. The dollar value of loans to date is $8,062,589.

Future plans include creating a microworking capital fund.

GHBDC'S annual operating budget is $370,000, and the loan capital fund is $5,174,000.

Note: Information as of 1992.

Hartford College for Women (HCW)
Entrepreneurial Center for Women
50 Elizabeth Street
Hartford, CT 06105
(203) 236-1215
FAX: (203) 233-5493
Contact: Donna Wertenbach

This college was founded in 1948, and the program was started in 1985 to help low- and moderate-income women and minorities procure self-employment as a viable economic option for achieving financial success.

The target population includes low- to moderate-income women and minorities throughout the state of Connecticut.

Technical assistance through business training courses includes individual business counseling, peer support and exchange, mentoring, networking, and marketing.

Financing is available to individual borrowers. Loan sizes range from $500 to $30,000, and the average loan is $15,000.

Agency achievements include Urban League Award—Partnerships for Parity and the Sex Equity Award, YWCA.

HCW's future plans include working with the unemployed/underemployed and expanding its mentor and marketing directory.

HCW's annual operating budget is approximately $150,000.

Note: Information as of 1992.

DELAWARE

No programs are indicated as of 1992.

GEORGIA

Greater Atlanta Small Business Project (GRASP)
Project Independence, Project New Ventures
10 Park Place South, Suite 305
Atlanta, GA 30303
(404) 659-5955
FAX (404) 880-9561
Contact: Maurice Coakley

This organization was started in 1986 as an "incubator without walls," assisting entrepreneurs to prepare for and compete in a dynamic market economy. GRASP assistance encompasses several elements, each vital to small business success: assessment of market potential, formal business training, facilitating access to financial resources, and providing technical assistance. The most unique aspect of GRASP is providing ongoing management support and mentoring for each client business. GRASP is also designed to bring targeted areas and minority individuals into the mainstream of small business development.

The target population is poverty-level, homeless, and unemployed individuals in the greater Atlanta metropolitan area.

Technical assistance includes business training courses; individual business counseling; peer support and exchange; mentoring; and financing, marketing, and procurement assistance.

Financing is for individual borrowers. Loan sizes range from $2,000 to $10,000, and the average loan is $5,000. Loan terms range from six months to two years, with the average term being one year. Interest rates vary from 2 to 5 percent.

Nonbusiness support services include individual counseling, child care, and transportation.

Agency achievements include the following: In 1988, the Council for Urban Economic Development recognized GRASP as one of "America's most successful economic development programs." In 1989, the U.S. Economic Development Administration included GRASP in its "Success Stories on Parade: America's Most Innovative and Imaginative Economic Development Programs." In 1991, GRASP's Market Smart program received the Minority Business Development Program of the Year award.

Future plans include expanding the small business incubator division and providing GRASP's goods and services to mainstream businesses for a fee.

The annual operating budget is $1 million, and the loan capital fund is $500,000.

Note: Information as of 1992.

HAWAII

No programs are indicated as of 1992.

IDAHO

No programs are indicated as of 1992.

ILLINOIS

Community Workshop on Economic Development (CWED)
100 South Morgan
Chicago, IL 60607
(312) 243-0249
FAX (312) 243-7796
Contact: Carol Hall

This organization started in 1982 as a coalition of community-based organizations, technical assistance providers, and individuals who organized to promote community-controlled economic development in Chicago's low-income communities, through equity-owned businesses called Community Ventures.

The target population is low-income, underemployed, or unemployed persons throughout the state of Illinois, but primarily Chicago and the surrounding suburbs.

Technical assistance provided includes business training courses, individual business counseling, peer support and exchange, and mentoring.

CWED achievements include assisting in 30 community ventures, working with the Cook County Department of Planning, and development of Technical Assistance to Business (TAB) groups and the Empowerment Zones programs.

Illinois Department of Commerce and Community Affairs
Self-Employment Training Program (SET)
620 East Adams Street
Springfield, IL 62701
(217) 524-6665
FAX (217) 785-6454
Contact: Larry Masterson

This organization, begun in July 1990, targets unemployed and underemployed Illinois residents and currently has 26 training sites throughout Illinois.

Technical assistance provides overall management and the coordination of training sites.

Achievements include the founding of over 300 new small businesses in Illinois by agency graduates.

Future plans include working to establish loan fund/seed capital for these high-risk graduates.

The annual operating budget is $1 million.

Note: Information as of 1992.

Self-Employment Research Project (SERP)
Roosevelt University
Economics Department
430 South Michigan Avenue
Chicago, IL 60605
(312) 549-2545
Contact: Steven Balkin

This agency was founded in 1987 to engage in research on the topic of self-employment, targeting the most disadvantaged poor people. It is currently working in the state of Illinois; however, SERP is open to the entire United States.

Achievements include winning the Burlington Northern Faculty Achievement award for research on issues relating to self-employment for the poor. SERP organized the Chicago Self-Employment Program Network and produced its directories. A book, Self-Employment for Low-Income People (Praeger-Greenwood, 1989), is published, along with numerous articles, reports, monographs, and editorials advocating for the low-income self-employed.

Future plans include developing a self-employment training program for inmates in prisons, generating self-employment assistance programs and policy targeted to the homeless, and performing research on international comparative public policy for the microenterprise sector.

The annual operating budget ranges from $3,000 to $50,000. Funding sources are foundations, as well as state and federal grants.

Note: Information as of 1992.

Small Business Development Center (SBDC)
Self-Employment Training (SET) Program
Southern Illinois University at Carbondale
Carbondale, IL 62901
(618) 536-2424
Contact: Judy Bartels

This agency was founded in 1987, under the Illinois Department of Commerce and Community Affairs, to provide entrepreneurial training to unemployed and underemployed people in the lower 16 counties of Illinois. In addition, it provides ongoing counseling and assistance to start-up businesses.

Technical assistance provided includes individual business counseling, and peer support and exchange.

During the last four years, this program supported over 90 start-ups and intends to put more emphasis on dislocated workers.

The annual operating budget is $90,000.

Note: Information as of 1992.

Uptown Center Hull House
Economic Development Unit
4529 North Beacon Street
Chicago, IL 60640
(312) 561-3500
FAX (312) 561-3507
Contact: Curtis Roeschley

This organization began as Uptown Center Hull House in 1963. The Economic Development Unit (EDU) began in 1986 as an umbrella under Hull House Association. The purpose is to serve as a community-based social service organization that offers a variety of programs responding to the needs of low- and moderate-income people in the north Chicago area.

Technical assistance includes individual business counseling, peer support and exchange, and business training courses.

Since July 1986, the program has offered small business counseling, serving over 100 people annually. Since December 1986, it has offered small business workshops, which now number nine annually. In November 1988, EDU started the fourth world artisans cooperative, which has over 100 artisans and craft people as members.

Since February 1989, EDU has held self-employment training classes for over 100 students to compile business plans.

Future plans include a real estate development project as a joint venture with a private developer to develop a site in the neighborhood for mixed use with both retail and office space. EDU has applied to the state to become a small business center on the north side of Chicago. It is also discussing with the city the possibility of establishing a revolving loan pool for eligible candidates.

The annual operating budget is $400,000 for Economic Development Unit.
Note: Information as of 1992.

Women's Self-Employment Project (WSEP)
Entrepreneurial Training Program
Group Lending Program
166 West Washington, Suite 730
Chicago, IL 60613
(312) 606-8255
FAX (312) 606-9215
Contact: Beverly Smith

This agency was established to assist low- and moderate-income women in the metropolitan Chicago area to achieve self-sufficiency through a strategy of self-employment.

Technical assistance includes a business training program, individual business counseling, and self-employment workshops.

Financing is available to individual borrowers and groups. For individuals and for groups, loan sizes range from $100 to $10,000. First-time borrowers are eligible for $1,500. The average loan size is $900 for first-time borrowers. Loan terms typically range 30, 60, and 90 days up to one year. The average loan term is one year.

Nonbusiness support referral service is offered.

Other elements of the program include mandatory savings and checking accounts, industry-specific workshops, advanced business training, clinics, and so forth.

Achievements include serving over 2,200 women through its employment "Bright Idea" workshop. Over 663 women participated in the entrepreneurial training program through which over 250 microbusineses were established.

WSEP plans to develop a membership association to further assist women to collectively reduce costs, increase production, and increase incomes. WSEP will continue policy work to impact legislation through documenting welfare demonstration projects.

The annual operating budget is $600,000, and the loan capital fund is $155,000. Funding sources are PRIs, grants, contracts, and earned income.
Note: Information as of 1992.

Wright College
Self-Employment Training Project (SET)
3400 North Austin
Chicago, IL 61201
(312) 794-3300
FAX (312) 794-3207
Contact: Anita Zurawsi

This agency was started in 1989 as an umbrella organization of Wright College, of the City Colleges of Chicago, to serve the Austin community members by offering them a variety of programs to assist in achieving their educational, career, and entrepreneurial goals while operating in a fiscally responsible manner to the benefit of the participants and the college.

Technical assistance includes self-employment training, individual business counseling, and peer support and exchange at monthly network meeting.

Wright's SET project, a division of Wright College Economic Development, graduated 33 participants with 11 new business start-ups in 1990 through 91.

Future plans include a resource library stocked with various types of information, including books, business plan outlines, loan package resources with availability to entrepreneurs, and also an incubator for small businesses/start-ups.

The annual operating budget is approximately $80,000.

Note: Information as of 1992.

YWCA
Women's Economic Ventures Enterprise (WEVE)
229 16th Street
Rock Island, IL 61201
(309) 788-9793
Contact: Lynn Spaight

This agency was started in 1990 as an umbrella organization under National YWCA to assist low- to moderate-income women in the Quad Cities metro area (Rock Island County) and Davenport, Iowa (Scott County), residents in achieving economic self-reliance through the development and/or expansion of small business.

Technical assistance includes business training programs, individual business counseling, peer support and exchange, and mentoring.

Financing is available to individual borrowers. Loan sizes range from $50 to $3,000. Loan terms range from six months to four years.

Nonbusiness support services include child care, transportation, and in-home classes for physically disabled persons.

Another element of the program is the Women's Business Council, networking organizations for women business owners.

WEVE's annual operating budget is $30,000 to $50,000. The loan capital fund is $10,000. Funding sources are CDBG, the SBA, matching private individuals and foundations, the Loan Capital Fund, and banks.

Note: Information as of 1992.

INDIANA

Eastside Community Investments Inc.
Self-Employment Loan Fund
Eastside Day Care Homes Cooperative
Revolving Loan Fund
3228 East 10th Street
Indianapolis, IN 46201
(317) 637-7300
Contact: Linda Gilkerson

This agency was founded in October 1991 to create jobs and improve the quality of housing on the near east side of Indianapolis, targeting low-income individuals, dislocated workers, and public-assistance recipients.

Technical assistance includes business training courses, individual business counseling, peer support and exchange, and mentoring.

Loans to individual borrowers range from $1,000 to $10,000.

Achievements include development of a 40-acre industrial park, now filled with 30 businesses that have created over 1,000 jobs. The program developed a fund for venture capital and self-employment, a revolving loan fund for small businesses, and a credit union. Eastside Community Investments, Inc., also initiated numerous community development housing projects and a group loan program focusing on investing in land, buildings, people, and industries.

The annual operating budget is $3,700,000, and the loan capital fund is $700,000. Funding sources include C.S. Mott Foundation, state loans, the Loan Fund for the Common Good, HUD Neighborhood Development Demonstration, other foundations, government, churches, individuals, corporations, and earned income.

Note: Information as of 1992.

IOWA

Institute for Social and Economic Development (ISED)
1901 Broadway, Suite 313
Iowa City, IA 52240
(319) 338-2331
FAX (319) 338-5842
Contact: John Else

This agency was founded in October 1987 to facilitate the empowerment of low-income people, women, minorities, and other disadvantaged persons through the integration of social and economic development strategies in planning, research, training, and technical assistance.

The geographic areas targeted are primarily Iowa and western Illinois; however, ISED does some national and international consultation.

Technical assistance includes business training courses, individual business counseling, peer support and exchange, mentoring, and facilitating loans from commercial banks and state loan funds.

ISED facilitates loans from commercial lenders for borrowers and provides partial loan guarantees; banks administer the loans. Loan sizes range from $800 to $70,000. The median loan is $5,000. Loan terms range from one to four years, and the average term is two years.

Nonbusiness support services include child care via JOBS program, transportation via JOBS program, and family development services via community agencies.

The annual operating budget is $750,000, and the loan capital fund is $200,000. Funding sources include state and federal grants/contracts, foundations, corporations, and civic and religious organizations.

Note: Information as of 1992.

Iowa Department of Economic Development
Self-Employment Loan Program (SELP)
Small Business Helpline
200 East Grand
Des Moines, IA 50309
SELP (515) 242-4793
Helpline (800) 532-1216 (in-state only)
(515) 242-4758
FAX (515) 242-4749
Contact: Burt Powley (SELP)
Toni Hawley (Small Business)

This organization was founded in 1986 to increase the economic wealth of Iowans through the expansion and diversification of the state's economy.

The target population is Iowa residents at least 18 years old with no more than 70 percent of the current lower living-standard income level. A helpline is available for those considering opening a new small business and for existing small businesses in the state of Iowa.

Technical assistance includes business training courses and individual business counseling.

Financing is offered to individual borrowers. Loan sizes range up to $5,000, with an average loan of $4,700. Loan terms are up to five years, and the average term is 52 months.

Agency achievements include a number one ranking in economic development policy in Center for Economic Development's "Report Card of the States" and a SELP-program loss rate of less than 40 percent.

Future plans include investment in human capital and capacity building and a move toward demand rather than supply-side programming. SELP also plans to raise income guidelines to include working poor and raise guideline amounts to $7,500.

The annual operating budget for SELP is $220,000, and the loan capital fund is $170,000.

Note: Information as of 1992.

KANSAS

No program information is indicated.

KENTUCKY

Human Economic Appalachian Development Corp. (HEAD)
HEAD Community Loan Fund
P.O. Box 504
Berea, KY
(606) 986-3283
FAX (606) 986-9494
Contact: Jann Yankauskas
              Reid Livingston

This agency was started in April 1987 as an umbrella organization of HEAD Corporation Community Loan Fund, which provides loans and technical assistance to individuals and/or community organizations starting or expanding micro- and small businesses or doing community development projects throughout central Appalachian communities.

The target population is low- to mid-income-level individuals who have been denied credit from traditional sources in the central Appalachian region, which includes eastern Kentucky, northeastern Tennessee, southwest Virginia, West Virginia, southeast Ohio, and northeast North Carolina.

Technical assistance includes individual business counseling, peer support and exchange, mentoring, and business plan development and mentoring assistance referral.

Financing is given to individual and group borrowers. The loan size for individuals ranges from $1,000 to $130,000, with an average loan size of $12,000 to $15,000. Individual loan terms range from one to five years, and the average term is three years.

For group borrowers, the loan size ranges from $500 to $5,000, and the average group loan is $4,700. Loan terms range from six months to three years. The average term is two years.

Nonbusiness support services include child care, transportation, and individual counseling.

Other elements of the program give borrowers access to Central Appalachian People's Federal Credit Union (CAPFCU) and to financial planning, also through CAPFCU.

Achievements include developing the Eastern Kentucky Child Care Coalition, providing loans to over 50 borrowers throughout the region, and producing the Access to Capital Project in 1991.

Future plans are to expand viability throughout the region through development of regionally based "loan committees" and "borrower groups." This is an effort to make capital and technical assistance more accessible and to promote locally controlled decision making about local resources needed.

The annual operating budget is $80,956, and the loan capital fund is $114,409.39.

Note: Information as of 1992.

LOUISIANA

No program information is indicated as of 1992.

MAINE

Aroostook County Action Program (ACAP)
Main Job Start Program
P.O. Box 1116
Presque, ME 04769
(207) 764-3721
FAX (207) 768-3022
Contact: Brian Tebow
        Connie Sandstrom

This agency was founded in October 1984 to establish a revolving loan fund for low-income individuals interested in starting or expanding a small business. It operates within the employment and training division of the Aroostook County Action Program, along with two CAP agencies in the state. The Finance Authority of Maine manages the loan fund.

Technical assistance and small business training are offered to improve the success rate of these businesses and to enable them to become bankable at a future date.

The target population is households with annual incomes of less than 80 percent of federal Housing and Urban Development median income guidelines in the state of Maine.

Technical assistance includes business training courses, individual business counseling, technical assistance to the public, and private agencies.

Financing is given to individual borrowers. Loan sizes range from $1,500 to $10,000. The average loan is $7,000. Loan terms range from 2 to 10 years, and the average term is 4.5 years. The interest rate is 2 percent below prime.

Nonbusiness support services include individual counseling, self-esteem building and training, follow-up on business progress, and referrals to other support services.

ACAP implemented a revolving loan concept for small or microbusiness development. This is the first time the state has committed to such an enterprise. ACAP established a partnership with the state's Finance Authority.

ACAP demonstrated effectiveness at providing small business training and enhanced technical assistance to prospective borrowers; it plans to continue these services as well as possibly initiating a support group in relation to training classes and future business support.

The annual budget is $30,000 for technical assistance. The loan capital fund is $284,000.

Coastal Enterprises, Inc. (CEI)
Water Street
P.O. Box 268
Wiscasset, ME 04578
(207) 882-7552
FAX (207) 882-7308
Contact: Ron Phillips

This organization was founded in 1977 to help Maine residents with low incomes reach an adequate and equitable standard of living, learning, and working by providing financial and technical assistance for small businesses in industry, social services, and housing development and through research and policy development.

The target population is low-income women, children, families, unemployed and self-employed persons, and welfare recipients, including AFDC recipients, people with disabilities, refugees, and those at risk of poverty throughout the state of Maine.

Technical assistance provided includes individual business counseling and workshops with CEI Small Business Development Center, packaging assistance for bank loans, customized clinics for specific populations or industries—for example, family child care providers, peer support and exchange, business training courses, clinics, workshops, and mentorships coordinated with Displaced Homemakers Project and Women's Business Development Corporation.

Financing is via guarantees for individual borrowers under the Enterprise Development Fund (EDF). Loan sizes range from $500 to $50,000. The average loan is $10,000. EDF guarantees 50 percent of bank loans up to $50,000. Loan terms are flexible, from one to five years, and the average guarantee is five years.

CEI operates three other funds: the Development Fund, the Housing Fund, and the Venture Capital Fund, with varying loan criteria and higher ranges of financing.

Nonbusiness support services include child care and transportation, coordinated with the Department of Human Services and employment training organizations. Employment development plans are created for job-generating companies receiving loans.

Coastal Enterprises is dedicated to improving sectoral intervention strategies in natural resource industries such as the fisheries; manufacturing and service businesses; social services, such as family and center-based child care; venture capital for innovative, job-generating, start-up and expanding firms; and small and microenterprise development, including women's business development.

Coastal Enterprises plans to expand finance and technical assistance in areas targeted to women and welfare recipients and to economic collaborative strategies to further develop social services areas, such as elderly care, supported and cooperative housing for single parents and low-income families, and independent residential living for the mentally retarded.

The annual budget is $1,400,000. The overall loan capital fund is $12,000,000. Two million dollars of this is for the Enterprise Development Fund. Funding sources include federal and state governments, churches, foundations, private banks, businesses, and income from loans.

Maine Displaced Homemakers Program
New Ventures Self-Employment Training for Women
Stoddard House, UMA
Augusta, ME 04330
(207) 621-3432
FAX (207) 621-3116
Contact: Eloise Vitelli

This organization was founded in 1984 to help prepare disadvantaged women to participate fully in the state's changing economy through innovative preemployment and self-employment training and support services.

The target population is displaced homemakers, welfare recipients, unemployed insurance recipients, dislocated workers, and single parents throughout the state of Maine.

Technical assistance includes business training courses, new ventures and introductory workshops, individual business consultation, peer support and exchange, information, and referral advocacy.

Nonbusiness support services are child care support dollars and advocacy, transportation support dollars and advocacy, career life planning, assertiveness, self-esteem, and economic awareness training support for the divorce process.

This is the only program in the state to consistently provide quality, long-term self-employment training to disadvantaged women. The program developed and is now marketing a model management information system that tracks participant demographics, services received, and outcomes, as well as playing a major role in founding another organization, WBDC, which operates a mentoring program. New Ventures has also helped develop and expand collaborative relationships among other agencies in the state working to support microenterprise development.

The program piloted, and will continue to offer, an economic awareness training and rural leadership development program to the target population. It also plans to develop work-force literacy training that incorporates entrepreneurship skills, and it is committed to strengthening partnerships and expanding the role of women in economic development.

The annual operating budget is $762,000.

Note: Information as of 1992.

MASSACHUSETTS

Hilltown Community Development Corporation
Hilltown Enterprise Fund
P.O. Box 17
Chesterfield, MA 01012
(413) 296-4536
Contact: Katheryn Woo

This organization was founded in 1981 to promote rural cooperation as a way to ensure the best quality of life for all Hilltown residents. The purpose is to enable people to help themselves in addressing local economic, housing, and social needs and to create and expand opportunities for those with limited resources.

The target population is individuals with limited resources who wish to start or expand a business located in Chesterfield, Chester, Cummington, Goshen, Huntington, Middlefield, Plainfield, Westhampton, Williamsburg, and Worthington, Massachusetts.

Technical assistance includes business training courses and workshops, individual business counseling, a business directory, and a resource library.

Financing is given to individual borrowers. Loan sizes range from $500 to $5,000. The average loan is $3,500. Loan terms range from six months to three years, and the term average is two years.

Future plans include increasing the loan pool to accommodate larger loans for longer terms.

The annual operating budget is $60,000, and the loan capital fund is $75,000.

Sources of funding include individuals, the Western Massachusetts Enterprise Fund, donations, income, and state and federal grants.

Note: Information as of 1992.

Management and Community Development Institute
Lincoln Filenes Center
Tufts University
Medford, MA 02155
(617) 381-3549
FAX (617) 381-3401
Contact: Mary Cronin

This agency was established in 1983 to build the capacity of community-based development organizations through staff and board training.

The target market is the staff and board members of community-based organizations nationwide, but primarily in New England.

Technical assistance includes business training courses, individual business counseling, and mentoring.

The agency has trained thousands of community developers and activists throughout the United States and Canada over the last 10 years.

Future plans are to extend training opportunities.

The funding sources are corporations and foundations.

Note: Information as of 1992.

Massachusetts Department of Employment and Training
The Enterprise Project
19 Staniford Street
Fourth Floor, Hurley Building
Boston, MA 02114
(617) 727-1826
FAX (617) 727-8014
Contact: Bonnie Dallinger

This agency was founded in March 1990 as an umbrella organization under the Federal Unemployment Insurance Self-Employment Demonstration Project.

The target population is newly unemployed people eligible for unemployment insurance benefits who are Massachusetts residents.

Technical assistance includes a business development seminar, workshops, individual business counseling, and peer support and exchange.

Financing is for individual borrowers. Loans are granted by private banks in partnership with the project. Loan sizes range from $2,000 to $60,000.

Nonbusiness support services include the Federal Worksearch Waiver, a program that allows participants to collect unemployment insurance benefits without having to look for work.

The annual operating budget is $240,000. The Department of Labor is the funding source for the operating budget.

Note: Information as of 1992.

Neighborhood Reinvestment Corporation
Commercial and Economic Development Department
Neighborhood Enterprise Center Program (NEC)
80 Boylston Street, Suite 1207
Boston, MA 02116
(617) 565-8240
FAX (617) 565-8452
Contact: Peg Barringer

This organization was founded in 1978. The NEC program started in 1989 as an umbrella organization to Neighborworks Network. The purpose of the Neighborhood Reinvestment program is to revitalize declining neighborhoods through the development and support of local public and private partnerships. The Commercial and Economic Development Department focuses on low- and moderate-income areas, to reverse the outflow of employment and investment capital; expand business development opportunities; and create a community of choice within which to live, work, and conduct business. The goal of the NEC program is to encourage enterprise development within disadvantaged populations in Jackson, Mississippi; West Philadelphia, Pennsylvania; Pasadena, California; and the Rosebud Reservation, South Dakota.

The target population is low-income people, women, and minorities.

Technical assistance includes business training courses, peer support and exchange, and assistance in improving access to markets.

Financing is given to group borrowers. Loan sizes range from $500 to $2,000. The average loan size is $1,000. Loan terms range from 4 to 12 months, and the average term is 9 months.

In addition to the NEC program, Neighborhood Reinvestment's other economic development programs have resulted in $2.3 million in loans made for CED projects; 219 businesses created or expanded (52 percent minority- or women-owned); 319 commercial buildings restored or constructed; 1,784 jobs created; and $111 million reinvested in business, commercial buildings, and infrastructure in declining areas.

The annual operating budget includes: Neighborhood Reinvestment, $20 million; the Commercial and Economic Development Department, $400,000; and each NEC, $50,000 to $70,000. The loan capital fund is $50,000 to $100,000 each. The funding sources are: the loan capital fund, lines of credit from local banks; the operating budget, Levi Strauss, C.S. Mott Foundation, Threshold, CDBG, and local banks.

Note: Information as of 1992.

Valley Community Development Corporation
Valley CDC Enterprise Fund
16 Armory Street
Northampton, MA 01060
(413) 586-5855
FAX (413) 585-0471
Contact: Christopher Sikes

This agency, established in September 1988, targets low- to moderate-income persons and minorities in western Massachusetts.

Technical assistance includes individual business counseling, peer support and exchange, and mentoring.

Financing is given to individual and group borrowers. Individual loan sizes range from $500 to $5,000, with an average of $4,000. Individual loan terms are from six months to three years.

For group borrowers, loan sizes range from $500 to $5,000, with an average of $500. Loan terms are from six months to three years.

Nonbusiness support services include individual counseling.

Achievements include creation of a regionwide loan fund with $150,000 in assets. The program has loaned successfully to businesses with 25 people employed.

Future plans are to create a venture capital fund to start businesses that are sold to the employees.

The annual operating budget is $385,500, and the loan capital fund is $70,000.

Sources of funding include the Western Mass Enterprise Fund and state and federal grants.

Note: Information as of 1992.

The Western Massachusetts Enterprise Fund (WMEF)
324 Wells Street
Greenfield, MA 01301
(413) 774-4204
Contact: Kathryn Woo

This agency was founded in 1990 to develop resources to support and increase the capacity of local community development corporations to invest capital in, as well as to provide technical assistance to, lower-income and minority enterprises and to create a climate of economic opportunity in the region. The goal is to promote alternative models for financing microenterprises and to promote greater responsiveness to community and low-income needs on the part of conventional lending institutions.

The target population is disadvantaged entrepreneurs in communities served by local nonprofit community development corporations in western Massachusetts.

Achievements include The Western Massachusetts Enterprise Fund. The model is now replicated via an agency in another part of the state. WMEF support enabled one CDC to start the first peer lending program in the state.

Future plans include continuing to develop resources for local microenterprise revolving loan and technical assistance programs.

WMEF's annual operating budget is $75,000.

Note: Information as of 1992.

MICHIGAN

Ann Arbor Community Development Corporation
Women's Initiative for Self-Employment (WISE)
2008 Hogback Road, Suite 2A
Ann Arbor, MI 48105
(313) 677-1400
Contact: Michelle Vasquez
          Sharon Peterson

This agency was founded in July 1984 to create and encourage small business development among women, minorities, people with disabilities, and other low-income residents in Ann Arbor.

The target population is primarily low-income residents of Washtenaw County, Michigan.

Technical assistance includes business training assistance, individual business counseling, peer support and exchange, business networking, and group services.

Financing is for individual borrowers, specifically for small business loans and capital leasing. Loan sizes range from $500 to $25,000, with an average of $7,000. Loan terms range from six months to five years. The average term is four years. The interest rate is prime plus 2 percent.

Nonbusiness support services include individual counseling, child care stipends, transportation stipends, and credit counseling.

Achievements include building the Community Loan fund for small businesses, the Black Business Directory, the Capital Leasing Program, the WISE Directory, and the Community Reinvestment Alliance and Welfare Rights of Washtenaw County.

The annual operating budget is $250,000, and the loan capital fund is $450,000.

Funding sources include Ann Arbor city, foundations, donations from members, federal grants, and county contracts.

Grand Rapids Opportunities for Women (GROW)
233 East Fulton, Suite 108
Grand Rapids, MI 49503

This organization was established in 1989 to enhance the environment of low-income women through advocacy, leadership development, and the promotion of economic self-sufficiency. GROW provides business training, mentor relationships, self-esteem building, and access to financing, targeting unemployed and underemployed women in Kent and Ottawa Counties of Michigan.

Financing is given to individual borrowers. Loan sizes range from $1,200 for first loans with a term of one year.

Nonbusiness support includes child care assistance and personal development sessions.

Achievements show that GROW graduated 28 people since training began in 1990. One woman has eight employees; three others are running full-time businesses, and all the others except two women are running part-time businesses.

Future plans include participating in statewide strategies to collaborate on programs such as bartering and technical assistance. In the future, GROW would also like to provide opportunities for women to open checking and savings accounts. GROW will contract with marketing and finance specialists to provide on-site consultation to GROW graduates.

GROW's annual operating budget is $120,000. The loan capital fund has a relationship with First Michigan Bank.

Note: Information as of 1992.

Handicapper Small Business Association (HSBA)
1900 South Cedar, Suite 112
Lansing, MI 48910
(517) 484-8440
Contact: Teresa Starkie

This agency was started in December 1987 as an umbrella organization to Specialty Center in the Michigan Small Business Development Center network to promote and facilitate entrepreneurship for people with disabilities. HSBA provides quality services to entrepreneurs with disabilities and rehabilitation professionals.

The target population is people with differing abilities and entrepreneurs with disabilities in any state, but primarily in Michigan.

Technical assistance includes business training courses offered at annual conference, individual business counseling for business start-ups, and peer support and exchange on a membership committee.

Achievements include advocating the passing of the Handicapper Business Opportunity Act (PA 112), which provides a 3 percent competitive opportunity in the state's procurement of goods, services, and construction contracts. HSBA formed several committees to advocate handicapper rights.

The business procurement committee is developing a strategy to encourage corporations, handicapper service organizations, and state agencies to do business with handicapper-owned firms.

Note: Information as of 1992.

Northern Economic Initiatives Corp.
Small Business Development Center
Field Services, Industry Services, Marketing Services
1500 Wilkinson
Marquette, MI 49855-5367
(906) 227-2406
FAX (906) 227-2413

This agency was founded in July 1985 on the premise that nothing so impacts the quality of life in a community as the health of its economy. In addition, it's believed that such an economy is best developed and transformed by enhancing the vitality of its import replacing and exporting firms most committed to growth. The goal is that this economic transformation should respect the rural character of its human settlements and the quality of the natural environment. The mission is to improve the competitive position of small Upper Peninsula firms by providing training, information, counseling, and encouragement. This group is formally affiliated with Northern Michigan University (NMU) and Shorebank Corporation.

The target population is small-product producers located in the Upper Peninsula of Michigan.

Technical assistance includes business training courses; individual business counseling on finances, production, marketing, and operations; peer support and exchange with industry networks; mentoring through the NMU alumni-mentoring program; and the Market Intelligence Program.

Financing is for individual borrowers. Loan sizes range from $300 to $20,000, with an average of $8,000. Loan terms range from one month to three years. The average term is nine months.

NEIC helps increase the survival rates and formation of viable microenterprises that replace imported products with local products. These firms typically employ fewer than 10 people, may be home based, and often involve family members. MEIC assists clients as they graduate from dependence on local markets to penetration of distinct export markets. Recent examples include successful product exhibitions in Detroit, New York, and Boston and merchandising of products in respected retail outlets. Many clients introduce new product innovations and manufacturing processes to meet demand; for example, a company has successfully integrated computer-aided design technology within a group of small woodworking firms.

This program has generated sales increases among clients and has spurred movement into new markets and investment in new technology as measures of success. To achieve these results, NEIC established a comprehensive database of 1,500 plus firms, their products, and, in some cases, their production capacities. Through conferences and consultations, over 400 firms per year have attended NEIC-sponsored events geared at developing a management capacity to begin production and respond to market demand. NEIC is achieving scale by shifting services to groups of firms organized to solve common problems. These industrial consortia interact with larger firms to respond flexibly to changes in technology and markets.

The annual operating budget is $708,000, and the loan capital fund is $232,500. Sources of funding are Joyce Foundation, the Michigan Department of Commerce, Michigan Research Excellence Fund, MISBDC of Wayne State University, Industrial Technology Institute, the Michigan Council of Arts, the Michigan Department of Agriculture, Ford Foundation, and private donations.

Note: Information as of 1992.

MINNESOTA

Northwest Area Foundation
West 975 First National Bank Building
332 Minnesota Street
St. Paul, MN 55101
(612) 224-9635
FAX (612) 298-9513

This organization was founded in October 1934 to contribute to the vitality of the region by promoting economic revitalization and improving the standard of living for the most vulnerable of its citizens.

The target population is low-income residents of Minnesota, Iowa, North Dakota, South Dakota, Montana, Idaho, Washington, and Oregon.

The foundation awarded 30 grants, totaling over $4.8 million, for projects demonstrating promising strategies for supporting small businesses.

The annual budget is $14,054,659; assets are $237 million. The source of funding is a private foundation.

Note: Information as of 1992.

Women Venture (formerly CHART/WEDCO)
Midtown Commons
2324 University Avenue
St. Paul, MN 55104
(612) 646-3808
FAX (612) 641-7223

This agency was founded to secure a stronger economic future for women through employment, career development, business development, and financial education, serving the seven-county area in Minneapolis/St. Paul.

Technical assistance includes individual business counseling.

Financing is given to individual borrowers. Loan sizes range from $500 to $5,000, with an average of $3,000. Loan terms are six months to three years.

The strategic plan outlines five crucial economic issues for the agency: women's entry into the work force, occupations and job segregation, growth opportunities for women-owned businesses, women's access to capital, and financial education.

The purpose of Project Blueprint is to recruit and train women in the construction trades and to provide passports to public housing residents to move toward finding a job, starting a business, or enhancing personal growth.

Note: Information as of 1992.

Northeastern Entrepreneur Fund, Inc.
Olcott Plaza
820 Ninth Street North
Virginia, MN 55792
(218) 749-4191
FAX (218) 741-4249
HandsNet: HN1155
Contact: Mary Mathews

This agency, begun in September 1989, is formally affiliated with Northeast Ventures Cooperation to foster an entrepreneurial spirit and encourage self-sufficiency through the growth of small-business and self-employment opportunities in the seven county Arrowhead Region, Northeastern Minnesota, targeting unemployed and underemployed men and women.

Technical assistance includes business training courses, individual business counseling, peer support and exchange.

Financing is to individual borrowers. Loan sizes range from $170 to $20,000. The average loan is $8,000. Loan terms range from 90 days to 3 years. The average loan term is three years.

The Access fund allows small grants to low-income customers to help defray some expenses during the business planning process.

The Northeast Entrepreneur Fund helped start or stabilize more than 65 small businesses in the first 19 months of operation.

The annual operating budget is $285,000, and the loan capital fund is $375,000. Sources of funding are foundations and corporations.

Note: Information as of 1992.

MISSISSIPPI

Friends of Children of Mississippi, Inc., Head Start
Self-Employment Investment Demonstration (SEID)
642 East Peace Street
Canton, MS 39046
(601) 859-5553
FAX (601) 362-1613

Contact: Marvin Hogan
        Glenda Crump
        W.H. Robinson

Friends of Children, Inc., was founded in 1968, and the SEID Program was begun in 1988 to empower and offer options to welfare recipients in rural Mississippi in an effort to assist them to become economically self-sufficient through self-employment.

Technical assistance includes business training courses, marketing and financial management, individual business counseling, peer support and exchange, a monthly borrower's meeting, and mentoring. Participants are matched with entrepreneurs.

Financing is given to individual borrowers. Loan sizes range from $50 to $2,000. The average loan is $1,700. Loan terms range from 24 to 30 months, and average term is 24 months.

Nonbusiness support services include individual counseling, child care stipends via the Jobs Program, transportation stipends, and car pooling arrangements. Other technical assistance is provided until the loan is paid in full.

Achievements include the 1991 JTPA Presidential Award for the top 10 outstanding training programs in the country, awarded by the U.S. Department of Labor.

Future plans are to exist beyond the initial demonstration, to provide assistance to low- and moderate-income men and women, and to expand the geographic area served.

The agency's annual operating budget is $4.5 million, and SEID's budget is $60,000. The loan capital fund is $37,500. Sources of funding include private foundations and a private industry council.

Note: Information as of 1992.

Mississippi Department of Economic and Community Development
Employment Training Division
Mississippi Service Delivery Area
P.O. Box 23669
Jackson, MS 39225-3669
(601) 949-2151
FAX (601) 949-2291
Contact: Geraldine Yates

The Mississippi Service Delivery Area (MSSDA) operates employment and training programs under Title II and Title III of the Job Training Partnership Act (JTPA). The mission of the MSSDA is to assist unskilled youths and adults and dislocated workers in obtaining employment and other services needed to qualify them for productive jobs.

The target population is welfare recipients and other economically disadvantaged and dislocated workers in the state of Mississippi.

The Welfare Self-Employment Initiative Demonstration program through Friends of Children in Canton, Mississippi, received a presidential award as an out-standing JTPA program.

The annual operating budget is $37,000,000 in JTPA Title II and III Funding.

Note: Information as of 1992.

Small Business Development Center of Mississippi Delta Community College

P.O. Box 5607
Greenville, MS 38704-5607
(601) 378-8133
Contact: Martha Heffner

This agency was established in October 1989 with a program designed to provide delivery of up-to-date counseling, training, and research assistance in all aspects of small business management. The program is for all persons interested in start-ing and maintaining a small business in the eight counties of the Mississippi delta.

Since starting this program, the agency has provided individual counseling to over 200 individuals and presented 20 seminars with over 400 people in attendance.

The annual operating budget is $65,000.

Note: Information as of 1992.

MISSOURI

Green Hills Rural Development, Inc.

Revolving Loan Fund
909 Main Street
Trenton, MO 64683
(816) 359-3069
FAX (816) 359-3096
Contact: Michael R. Johns

This organization was founded in 1981 to promote economic development, job creation, and private investment in a nine-county area of rural North Central Missouri.

Technical assistance includes individual business counseling.

Financing is for individual borrowers. Loan sizes range from $10,000 to $80,000, with an average loan of $25,000. Loan terms range from 4 to 10 years, and the average term is five years.

The Revolving Loan Fund enhances credit access for people not otherwise able to enter business for themselves.

There are plans to begin a new relending program and to try to double or triple the program's access to loan capital. The program would also like to use state tax credits to receive donations toward increasing the revolving loan fund capital.

The annual operating budget is $357,000, and the loan capital fund is $550,000. Sources of funding are the EDA Title IX loan fund and federal, state, and local sources.

Note: Information as of 1992.

MONTANA

Billings Area Business Incubator (BABI)
This agency is now operating under the Montana Trade Port Authority.
115 North Broadway, Suite 200
Billings, MT 59101-2043
(406) 256-6871
FAX (406) 256-6877
Contact: Jerry Thomas
         Robyn K. LaRango

This organization operates to promote regional economic development by assisting people in new and small businesses through basic technical assistance, education, consulting, and financial recommendations.

Technical assistance includes business training courses taught by local business people, individual business counseling, peer support and exchange, and mentoring.

Financing is provided through referrals to other agencies.

Women's Opportunity and Resource Development (WORD)
Women's Economic Development Group
127 North Higgins, Third Floor
Missoula, MT 59802
(406) 543-3550
FAX (406) 721-4584
Contact: Kelly Rosenleaf

This organization was founded in September 1986 to assist Montana men and women, particularly low-income, unemployed, and underemployed single parents, to achieve self-sufficiency through microbusiness ownership.

Technical assistance includes individual business counseling, workshops, and loan packaging.

Financing is given to individual borrowers. Loan sizes range up to $15,000, with an average of $11,000. Loan terms are up to five years.

Achievements include accessing public money, particularly the microbusiness development act that makes $3.4 million available to fund 10 loan programs in Montana.

Future plans include tourism business development and policy influence and possibly work with refugee population.

The annual operating budget is $130,000, and the loan capital fund is $350,000. Funding sources include the city of Missoula; the state of Montana; city, county, and state foundations; and client fees.

Note: Information as of 1992.

NEBRASKA

Center for Rural Affairs (CRA)
Rural Enterprise Assistance Project (REAP)
P.O. Box 405
Walthill, NE 68067
(402) 846-5428
FAX (402) 846-5428
Contact: Rose Jaspersen

The Center for Rural Affairs was founded in 1973, and REAP was begun in 1990 to provide small rural communities with appropriate small business support systems that enable current (and future) microbusiness owners to realize their full potential as self-employed individuals and as members of the community.

REAP provides small business loans linked with basic business training through locally organized associations that have access to a small revolving fund capitalized by local funds (25 percent) and REAP funds (75 percent).

The target population includes very small and start-up business owners in small rural communities in farm-based regions of the Midwest (currently Nebraska, Kansas, and surrounding states).

Technical assistance includes business training courses, including a four-session curriculum open to the public as well as to group members; peer support and exchange; mentoring arranged informally; and an introduction to other service providers.

Financing is for group borrowers. Loan sizes range from $100 to $10,000. Loan terms are from 6 to 24 months. Sixty-seven loans have been made to date. The dollar value of loans to date is in excess of $60,000. The interest rate is prime plus 4 percent.

Future plans include expanding associations serving many small communities; enhancing cost-effectiveness of the rural delivery system by local circulation of video tapes designed to educate and prime distant communities for organizing a REAP association; requiring local community groups to become even more involved; researching and designing an individual-based loan program; and developing follow-up business training.

Northeast Nebraska Economic Development District (NNEDD)
All Nebraska's Inventor's Fair
600 South 13th Street, #10
Norfolk, NE 68701
(402) 379-1150

This organization, founded in 1981, is committed to economic and community development.

Inventors in Nebraska are the target market.

Technical assistance includes business training courses, individual business consulting, peer support and exchange, mentoring, matching funds, and marketing.

Nonbusiness support services include individual counseling, technical assistance, and patent assistance.

Achievements include helping many inventors bring their inventions to the marketplace. In the future the organization hopes to broaden its base of support among helping agencies and to create stronger ties with manufacturers.

The annual operating budget is $20,000.

NEVADA

No programs are indicated as of 1992.

NEW HAMPSHIRE

Working Capital
2500 North River Road
Manchester, NH 03106
Phone: NH (603) 644-3124
FAX: (603) 644-3150
MA (617) 547-9109
FAX: (603) 876-8186
Contact: Jeffrey Ashe

This organization was founded in September 1990 as a program of the Institute for Cooperative Community Development (ICCD). ICCD is the nonprofit affiliate of the Community Economic Development Program of New Hampshire College.

Working Capital meets the needs of small self-employed business owners by offering them a flexible and growing line of business credit and a chance to meet and share ideas with other business owners.

Credit and other services are offered through business loan groups. Continued access to capital depends on the group being current with their loans.

The target population includes low- to moderate-income self-employed business owners living in low-income communities and small cities in New Hampshire, Vermont, and western Massachusetts.

Technical assistance extends to peer support and exchange.

Financing is for group borrowers. Loans are made to individuals as members of business loan groups. Loan sizes range from $500 to $1,500, with an average of $700. Loan terms range from four months to one year. The average term is six months.

Each group has a "group fund" to pay for late payments for members and eventually to use to make loans to group members. Some Enterprise agents arrange for speakers and other technical assistance directly. The program is carried out in the field by 12 local organizations, including community development corporations, community action agencies, a town government, a regional planning agency, a land trust, and a small enterprise program.

The annual operating budget is $135,000. The loan capital fund is a $200,000 line of credit to ICCD from banks participating in the project. Sources of funding include Ford Foundation, C.S. Mott Foundation, the U.S. Department of Health and Human Services, the New Hampshire Charitable Trust, and Sun-Microsystems.

NEW JERSEY

New Jersey Community Loan Fund
126 North Montgomery Street
Trenton, NJ 08608
(609) 989-7766
FAX (609) 353-9513

This organization was founded in 1987 to provide loans and technical assistance to community-based organizations and low-income cooperatives for housing and economic development projects benefiting lower-income people.

The target population includes low-income people and low-income communities in New Jersey.

Technical assistance includes financial and projects and organization assistance for housing and development projects.

Financing is given for cooperatives or nonprofits. Loan sizes range from $5,000 to $65,000, with an average of $20,000. Loan terms range from 30 days to five years. The average term is 24 months. The interest rate is below prime.

The annual operating budget is $120,000, and the loan capital fund is $480,000. Funding sources are institutional and individual investors, grants, donations, and earnings.

Note: Information as of 1992.

NEW MEXICO

Ganados Del Valle
P.O. Box 118
Los Ojos, NM 87551
Phone: (505) 588-7896/7231
FAX: (505) 588-9514
Contact: Maria Varela

This organization was founded in 1981 to revitalize the agricultural and cultural ecology of the Terra Amarilla.

The target population is members, employees, and contractors of Gandos, in Northern Rio Arriba County.

Technical assistance includes individual business counseling, peer support and exchange, product design, market development, and management problem solving.

Financing is for individual and group borrowers. Individual loan sizes range from $100 to $500, with an average of $300. Terms range up to two years. Group loan sizes range from $3,000 to $18,000, with an average of $16,000. Terms range up to eight years.

Ganados del Valle assisted in several business start-ups and provides a training program for Tierra Wools, a cooperative business.

Future plans include organizing borrowing groups in different villages.

The annual operating budget is from $270,000 to $325,000. The loan capital fund is $125,000. Sources of funding are grants.

Women's Economic Self-Sufficiency Team (WESST Corp.)
414 Silver SW
Albuquerque, NM 87102
Phone: (505) 848-4760
FAX: (505)848-2368 (Attn: WESST Corp.)
Contact: Joellyn K. Murphy

This organization was founded in 1988 to help women create their own economic security through business ownership. WESST Corp. empowers women by providing consultation, training, and financial assistance to any women interested in starting or expanding a business.

The target market is low-income, unemployed, and underemployed women in New Mexico.

Technical assistance includes individual business counseling, peer support and exchange, mentoring, workshops, financial counseling, and resource referral.

Financing is for individual borrowers. Loan sizes range from $250 to $5,000, with an average of $4,333. Loan terms are from one to five years, and the average term is three years.

Achievements include providing technical assistance and training to over 550 women through the business consulting series—twice the projected goals; establishing a revolving loan fund to improve capital access; and establishing outreach sites in Santa Fe and Taos, serving rural women. It has also established and facilitated the Personal Side of Business Workshop series to explore balance between business and personal lives, tripled its staff, and recruited over 40 volunteer businesspeople, lawyers, and accountants to provide pro bono client services.

Future plans are to continue providing business consulting services and workshops, offer the Personal Side of Business Workshop series on a continuing funded basis, revise the loan application requirements to encourage more requests, and establish outreach sites in rural New Mexico to serve women throughout the state.

The annual operating budget is $255,000. The loan capital fund is $105,000. Funding sources include Sisters of Charity, C.S. Mott Foundation, Levi Strauss, SBA-OWBO, foundations, corporations, and fee-for-service income.

Note: Information as of 1992.

NEW YORK

Alternatives Federal Credit Union
301 West State Street
Ithaca, NY 14850
Phone: (607) 273-4666
FAX: (607) 277-6391
Contact: William Meyers

This organization was founded in January 1979 to provide appropriately scaled, locally controlled community development in the form of financial services to low-income, self-employed, and nonprofit organizations.

The target population is small businesses with fewer than 12 employees and less than $1,000 in sales in Tompkins County and contiguous towns.

Technical assistance includes business training seminars, individual business financial analysis, peer support and exchange, and "roundtables."

Financing is given to individual and group borrowers. Individual loan sizes range from $1,000 to $100,000, with an average of $25,000. Terms range from three months to seven years, with an average of three years. Interest rates range from 6.25 percent to 11.5 percent. The number of loans to date is 5,520, with a dollar value of $39,000,000.

Group loan sizes range from $5,000 to $80,000, with an average of $55,000. Terms range from three to five years, with an average of three years. The interest rate is market rate.

Achievements include the Youth Enterprises Program (a mini-MBA for high school students), and the Support, Marketing, and Documenting Program. Three focus areas developed include: small businesses and home-based businesses for women and minorities; financial services and lending to nonprofits; and tax and loans (cash services) guarantees and letters of credit.

The annual operating budget is $1,500,000. The loan capital fund is $18,000,000.

Opportunity Resource Institute (ORI)

Minority and Women Business Enterprise Development Center
1831 Bathgate Avenue
Bronx, NY 10459
Phone: (212) 901-3500
FAX: (212) 299-6623

This organization was founded in 1986 to promote and create economic development and employment-generating opportunities within and for the benefit of low-income communities.

The target population is women and minorities in Bronx, Lower Westchester, and Upper Manhattan.

Technical assistance includes business training courses, individual business counseling, public and private loan packaging, peer support and exchange, and mentoring.

Financing for individual borrowers is guaranteed by ORI and granted by banks or credit unions. The maximum loan guarantee is $5,000.

Nonbusiness support services include general information and referral for services and assistance. ORI offers a fully furnished small business incubator for minority start-ups.

Achievements since 1989 include providing assistance for over 200 clients, helping 20 new business start-ups employing over 100 people; providing training and consulting to 40 existing businesses; and securing or committing over $1.5 million in direct loans and $450,000 in new contracts to ORI clients.

ORI plans to expand incubator support services, business training/world-of-work training for high school youths, day care center development, and job training for dislocated workers.

The annual operating budget is $490,000, and the loan capital fund is $40,000.

Note: Information as of 1992.

NORTH CAROLINA

Center for Community Self-Help/Self-Help Credit Union

413 East Chapel Hill Street
Durham, NC 27701
Phone: (919) 683-3016
FAX: (919) 688-3615
Contact: Katherine McKee

This organization was founded in 1980 to provide economic justice and opportunity for the economically disadvantaged throughout North Carolina. From its original focus on worker ownership, it has grown in size and scope, now providing financial and technical assistance to business and housing projects that address the economic needs of rural, minority, female, and low-income individuals across the state.

The center provides loan servicing to the North Carolina Rural Microenterprise Loan Program and coordinates the North Carolina Urban Microenterprise Loan Program.

The target population is low-income people, rural residents, minorities, and women in North Carolina.

Achievements include assisting in the design of the Rural Microenterprise Loan Program. It services all loans made under the program. Outside the Rural Microenterprise Loan Program, Self-Help has made over $650,000 in loans of under $35,000 since 1989.

Self-Help is initiating an urban microenterprise initiative to complement the North Carolina Rural Economic Development Center's Rural Microenterprise Program.

The annual operating budget is $519,000. The sources of funding are national and North Carolinian foundations and churches and revenues generated by lending activities.

MDC, Inc.
P.O. Box 2226
Chapel Hill, NC 27514
(919) 968-4531
FAX (919) 929-8557
Contact: Mary Mountcastle

This organization was established in 1987 as a private nonprofit research corporation, created to design and evaluate work-force and economic policies and programs. MDC works with government, business, educational institutions, and the nonprofit sector to design, implement, and assess innovative strategies in economic and work-force development.

The target population is primarily in the South.

Achievements include evaluation of North Carolina Rural Economic Development Center's Microenterprise Loan Fund Demonstration Program. It completed a 12-month interim report as well as a two-year review.

The annual operating budget is $843,000.

Black Mountain Microenterprise Fund
101 1/2 Cherry Street
Black Mountain, NC 28711
(704) 669-2632 or 669-5393
Contact: Christopher Just

This organization was founded in August 1989 to create and stabilize very small businesses or microenterprises through a program of financial assistance and ongoing technical assistance designed to improve economic conditions and opportunities in western North Carolina.

The target population is low- to moderate-income individuals, unemployed and underemployed minority individuals, and individuals involved in business who cannot receive financial assistance from traditional banking institutions in western North Carolina.

Sources of funding include the North Carolina General Assembly, the Rural Economic Development Center, and the Dogwood Fund.

Technical assistance provided includes business training courses, individual business counseling, peer support and exchange, mentoring, a newsletter, informal get-togethers and networking between businesses, and technical assistance providers.

Financing is given to group borrowers. Loan sizes range from $500 to $8,000 with an average of $2,600. Loan terms range from six months to two years, and the average term is one year.

Nonbusiness support services include development of a savings account program. Each borrower is required to set aside $2 per business per meeting and three percent of their loan.

The program wishes to serve specific target groups, such as minority women and more rural groups. Plans include a newsletter and expanding technical assistance.

The annual operating budget is $90,000, and the loan fund is $100,000.

North Carolina Rural Economic Development Center
North Carolina Microenterprise Loan Program
4 North Blount Street
Raleigh, NC 27601
(919) 821-1154
FAX (919) 834-2890
Contact: William Bynum

This program, begun in 1989, serves rural, low-income, minority, and female residents of 14 rural counties in North Carolina.

Technical assistance includes business training courses, individual business counseling, and peer support and exchange.

Financing is given to individual and group borrowers. Individual loan sizes range up to $20,000, with a term of three years.

Group loan sizes range up to $8,000, with an average of $2,540. The term is up to two years, with an average of 18 months.

Achievements include establishing three to five new lending sites.

The annual operating budget is $125,875, and the loan capital fund is $1.1 million. The Rural Center receives funding from the state of North Carolina that allows for its continuation and expansion; other sources of funding are foundations and the Rural Economic Development Center.

NORTH DAKOTA

North Dakota State Board for Vocational Education
Vocational Marketing Education
Small Business Management/Entrepreneurship
State Capital, 15th Floor
600 East Boulevard Avenue
Bismarck, ND 58505
(701) 224-3182
FAX (701) 224-3000

This organization was founded in 1960 to provide long-term educational assistance to small businesses in order to improve organizational, management, and operational skills. The educational program is designed to help provide the businessperson with an understanding of the unique aspects of his or her business and provide appropriate tools to render timely and competent management decisions.

The target population is small business owners and managers or those intending to be small business owners and managers in North Dakota.

Technical assistance includes business training courses.

The annual operating budget is $265,000. Funding sources are local, state, and federal vocational education funds.

OHIO

Women's Entrepreneurial Growth Organization
P.O. Box 544
Akron, OH 44309
(216) 535-9346
FAX (216) 535-4523
Contact: Barbara Honthumb Lange

This organization was founded in September 1988 to promote economic equality, opportunity, and financial self-sufficiency for women through small business and microenterprise development. It is affiliated with the Small Business Development Center and Women's World Banking.

The target population is low- to moderate-income women in Northeast Ohio.

Technical assistance includes individual business counseling, peer support and exchange, empowerment, and personal skills development.

Financing is provided for individual borrowers. Loan sizes range from $100 to $10,000.

The annual operating budget is $200,000, and the loan capital fund is $35,000. Grants are the source of funding.

OKLAHOMA

Cherokee Community Initiatives, Inc.
Cherokee Community Loan Fund
3050 South Muskogee
Tahleqah, OK 74464
(918) 456-0765
Contact: Bertha Alsenay

This organization was established in October 1990 to promote long-term, locally controlled economic development in rural Cherokee communities.

The target population is rural, isolated, low-income microenterprises and cottage industries in 14 northeast counties of Oklahoma.

Technical assistance includes individual business counseling, peer support and exchange, mentoring, and a resource library.

Financing is provided for individual borrowers. Loan sizes range from $500 to $1,500.

Future plans include expanding to form two circle lending groups per county by the end of five years.

The annual operating budget is $100,000. Sources of funding are grants from foundations.

OREGON

No programs are indicated as of 1992.

PENNSYLVANIA

Economic Opportunity and Training Center (EOTC)
Self-Employment Training
Jane Building, Suite 3-D
116 North Washington Ave.
Scranton, PA 18503
Contact: Sharon McCrone

This organization was founded in December 1987 to facilitate employment opportunities to individuals who need support and direction in becoming self-sufficient through employment and to provide employment and training support services to employers.

The target population is welfare recipients and unemployed and underemployed, and low-income people in Lackawanna County.

Technical assistance includes individual business counseling, peer support and exchange, mentoring, monitoring, and technical assistance for application to the revolving loan fund.

Financing is provided for individual borrowers. Loan sizes range from $3,000 to $7,500, with an average of $3,000.

Nonbusiness support services include child care, transportation, and employment-readiness training.

Achievements include an award of first-of-its-kind funding from Pennsylvania governor Robert P. Casey's Drug Policy Council and Advisory Council on young children, to provide drug and alcohol education to parents and children from birth to three years who live in the Scranton area housing projects. EOTC was awarded a contract to administer the Appalachian Regional Committee (ARC) revolving loan fund, and it participated with Philadelphia and Pittsburgh in a self-employment training pilot project. EOTC was chosen by the Pennsylvania Department of Public Welfare (DPW) to produce a parenting training syllabus and to conduct statewide in-service training for DPW case managers.

Future plans include expansion of employment readiness training to include a broader range of displaced homemakers and single parents, expansion of family matters to include pregnant and young parents, and joint ventures with Head Start.

The annual operating budget is $260,000, and the loan capital fund is $70,000. Sources of funding include the Appalachian Regional Committee and public and private sources.

Note: Information as of 1992.

RHODE ISLAND

No programs are indicated as of 1992.

SOUTH CAROLINA

No programs are indicated as of 1992.

SOUTH DAKOTA

The Lakota Fund
Circle Banking Project
P.O. Box 340
Kyle, SD 57752
(605) 455-2500
FAX (605) 455-2585

Contact: Elsie Meeks

This organization was established in June 1987 to support the development of private Lakota-owned and operated businesses on the Pine Ridge Indian Reservation by providing financial and technical assistance and fostering personal development.

The target population is the Oglala Lakota tribal members that reside on the Pine Ridge Indian Reservation of South Dakota.

Technical assistance includes business plan preparation, business training courses, personal effectiveness training, and peer support and exchange.

Financing is given to individual and group borrowers. Individual loan sizes range up to $10,000, with an average of $4,000. Loan terms range up to three years, with an average of two years.

Group loan sizes range up to $1,000, with an average of $375.

Nonbusiness support services include alcohol and drug awareness programs.

The Lakota Fund is developing a broad campaign to make going into business more attractive and developing marketing strategies for credit producers locally and outside the area in order to increase participation in the project.

The annual operating budget is $200,000, and the loan capital fund is $800,000. Sources of funding include program-related investments, grants, and loan interest income.

Note: Information as of 1992.

TENNESSEE

East Tennessee Community Design Center
Rural Connections Program
1522 Highland Avenue
Knoxville, TN 87916
(615) 525-9945
FAX (615) 522-6760
Contact: Saundra Swink

This organization was founded in 1987 to assist the low-income public and private nonprofit organizations with planning, design, and development projects through the use of pro bono professionals as technical advisers.

The target population is low-income, nonprofit organizations engaged in community economic development in 18 rural counties surrounding Knoxville, Tennessee.

Services provided include training in the business development process, networking among groups, technical assistance in support of the enterprise development process in each community, and the Micro Loan Fund.

The Micro Loan Fund provides loans up to $5,000 with money from Levi Strauss and First American National Bank.

Rural Connections completed a three-year Rural Community Economic Development Program that trained and provided technical assistance to five rural nonprofit, community-based organizations in Virginia, North Carolina, and Tennessee that created 25 businesses, providing 157 jobs. A second training cycle has produced 10 nonprofit groups in East Tennessee. The first session of the third training cycle for 10 nonprofit groups was held in March 1994; attendance by previous participants was encouraged.

The annual operating budget for ETCDC is $250,000. For Rural Connections, the budget is $137,000.

Matrix, Inc.
220 Carride Street
Knoxville, TN
(615) 525-6310
Contact: Kahla Gentry

This organization was founded in 1985 to assist and support the successful development of new businesses, particularly those owned by women and minorities, by promoting low-cost space, individual technical assistance, and training programs.

The target population is low-income women and minorities in Knox County and surrounding counties in East Tennessee.

Technical assistance includes an eight week business training course.

Twenty graduates are currently operating businesses. The successful development business incubator has several graduates.

Future plans include beginning a Women's World Bank loan guarantee program. Matrix is also considering beginning a peer-group lending program.

The annual operating budget is $80,000, and the loan capital fund is $5,000. Sources of funding are Levi Strauss Foundation, building management contracts, and JTPA contracts.

Note: Information as of 1992.

Tennessee Valley Authority (TVA)
Valley Resource Center
Minority Economic Development (MED)
Special Opportunities Counties (SOC)
Business River Development (BRD)
400 West Summit Hill Drive
Knoxville, TN 37902
MED (615) 632-4405 FAX (615) 632-3148
SOC (615) 632-3148 FAX (615) 632-6128
CRD (615) 632-6499 FAX (615) 632-7335
BRD (615) 632-3369 FAX (615) 632-7335

TVA began in 1933 to achieve a competitive regional economy by helping to strengthen local communities, upgrading the valley's human and natural resources, and supporting a more innovative private sector.

Target populations include MED: minority residents; SOC: the 50 poorest counties; CRD: communities and community organizations in a 201-county region, including all of Tennessee and parts of Kentucky, Georgia, North Carolina, Virginia, Alabama, and Mississippi.

The Minority Economic Development program provides individual business counseling, mentoring, support for creation of business incubators, support for minority purchasing councils, and special assistance to minority female heads of family.

Achievements include creation of a minority-oriented procurement program in the division of purchasing; creation of two MESBICs, eight revolving loan funds, and a $15 million regional loan fund; demonstration of youth entrepreneurship using business kids kits; female head-of-family demonstrations; establishment and support of minority supplier purchasing councils; and the tristate effort to match minority suppliers with NASA/Yellow Creek Construction project.

Future plans include a regional minority manufacturing and entrepreneurial center, a model youth entrepreneurial program, and a regional minority and economically disadvantaged business development fund.

The Special Opportunities Counties (SOC) program provides business counseling and financial analysis, as well as limited financing, for approved new or expanding businesses in SOC counties.

This program manages a $12 million revolving loan fund, serving new or expanding businesses in SOC areas. It also provides limited financing for approved infrastructure projects in SOC counties. It has limited experience in microloans, rural small business incubators, and school-based enterprises.

The Community Resource Development Program provides identification and preliminary packaging of business development projects for SOC funding.

Achievements include design and funding of a three-year training and technical assistance program for five CBOs in Central Appalachia undertaking housing and business development projects; assistance to the Tennessee Network for Community Economic Development (TNCED) in developing projects; and technical and financial assistance to a self-employment project for JPTA-eligible individuals in two rural counties in East Tennessee.

Future plans are to identify opportunities for self-employment/microenterprise development projects as part of an ongoing program. It also plans potential limited technical and financial assistance to start-up projects demonstrating an innovative approach in geographic areas targeted by TVA for development assistance.

The Business and River Development program provides individual business counseling. It was awarded the Mobile Small Business Assistance Center (MSBAC) Program Bronze award for excellence in economic development by the American Economic Development Council. Begun as a pilot program in Tennessee, it is now in eight southeastern states. Business incubator programs are funded in Mississippi, Alabama, Tennessee, and North Carolina.

Note: Information as of 1992.

TEXAS

No programs are indicated as of 1992.

UTAH

No programs are indicated as of 1992.

VERMONT

Central Vermont Community Action Council
Micro Business Development Program (MBDP)
P.O. Box 747
Barre, VT 05641
(802) 479-1053
FAX (802) 479-5353
Contact: Mary Niebling, director of Community Economic Development

This agency was founded in 1965, with the MBDP starting in 1978, to break the cycle of poverty by providing low-income Vermonters with the information, opportunities, education, and increased self-assurance they need to become self-sufficient. The MBDP offers free one-on-one technical assistance and business workshops to income-eligible Vermonters who want to start or expand businesses.

The target population is low-income Vermonters. Technical assistance includes business training courses and individual business counseling. The agency also provides access to the Vermont Job Start Individual Lending Program.

MBDP has assisted over 400 Vermonters since 1988. Over 100 people have received financing for business ventures.

MBDP plans to work even more closely with its clients on targeting, goal-setting, and problem solving, with more intensive support over a longer period of time.

The annual operating budget is $200,000. The loan capital fund of $250,000 is in partnership with the Vermont Job Start Loan Program.

City of Burlington Community and Economic Development Office (CEDO)
Burlington Revolving Loan Program
Women's Small Business Program Peer Lending Fund
Room 32, City Hall
Burlington, VT 05401
(802)865-7144
FAX (802) 865-7024
Contact: Bruce Seifer

This organization was founded in 1983 to target disadvantaged neighborhoods, low- and moderate-income men, women, and minorities in Burlington, Vermont, and northwest Vermont, depending on the program and funding source.

Technical assistance includes business training courses, individual business counseling, peer support and exchange, a research library, and incubator development.

Financing is for individual and group borrowers. Individual loan sizes range from $4,000 to $55,000, with an average of $12,500. Loan terms range from one to seven years, with an average term of four years.

The group loan size is $500, with a term of four months.

Nonbusiness support services include individual counseling for women in the business program, child care for women in the business program, and transportation for women in the program.

CEDO, through its Burlington Revolving Loan Program, provided technical assistance to over 1,000 small businesses and made 15 loans to small businesses, resulting in the creation of over 160 jobs. CEDO's Women's Small Business Project provided business orientation to 400 women and comprehensive business skill training and technical assistance to 90 women. CEDO was involved in drafting legislation to provide loans through the Vermont Industrial Development Authority for amounts up to $200,000 for the development of small business incubators.

The annual budget is $300,000, and the loan capital fund is $50,000. Funding sources include the Community Development Block Grant and payback.

Northeast Employment and Training Organization
Employment thru Proprietorship (ETP)
P.O. Box 584
Newport, VT 05855
or
Ridge View 91 Derby Road
Derby, VT
(802) 334-8148
Contact: Kay Lafoe

This organization was founded in 1979 with the goal to give people the educational training and skills to allow them to become self-supporting and not reliant on welfare benefits.

The target population is low-income people, long-term welfare recipients, long-term unemployed persons, offenders, and displaced homemakers in eight counties in northern Vermont.

Technical assistance includes business training courses, a 12-credit entrepreneurial course, individual business counseling, peer support and exchange, forums with previous students, and an advisory board review and critique of completed business plans.

Nonbusiness support includes child care via the Department of Social Welfare, transportation via carpooling, and individual counseling.

Achievements include the development and implementation of the first U.S. college-credited entrepreneurial certificate program dealing solely with welfare recipients, displaced homemakers, and long-term unemployed persons. This was implemented in 1986 and won the NADO Award (National Alliance of Development Organizations) for excellence in 1987. This program served as a model for the General Electric Retraining for Laid-off Workers Program that was copied by many states. In September 1991, NEI was awarded honorable mention for the Governor's Award for excellence in employment and training for the top adult program of the year.

ETP was awarded a grant that will allow it to work with people 55 or older in retraining and learning new skills.

The annual operating budget is $30,000. The sources of funding are the Vermont Department of Employment and Training and the Vermont Department of Education.

Note: Information as of 1992.

State Economic Opportunity Office
Vermont Job Start
102 South Maine Street
Waterbury, VT 05671-1801
(802) 241-2450
FAX (802) 244-8103
Contact: Tom Schroeder

This agency was founded in October 1978, under the Agency of Human Services, as an economic development program aimed at increasing self-employment opportunities for low-income Vermonters. Job Start loans are available to start, strengthen, or expand small businesses.

The target population is single people with an adjusted gross income of less than $14,000 and up-to-six-person families with adjusted gross incomes of less than $24,000 throughout the state of Vermont.

Technical assistance includes business training courses with 12 hours of classroom time, individual business counseling, and one-on-one training as needed.

Financing is given to individual borrowers. Loan sizes range from $1,000 to $10,000, with an average of $4,500. Loan terms range from one to four years. The average term is three years. Other public and private funding resources are also recommended.

Vermont Job Start maintains a technical assistance staff through state general funds and federal grants for business training. It has secured additional loan capital for relending from J.C. Penney Life Insurance.

Vermont Job Start plans to secure a consistent source of capital for relending, to negotiate with banks for lines of credit, and to broaden income guidelines to correct for inflation.

The annual operating budget is $40,000. The funding source is interest income from loans. The loan capital fund is in excess of $240,000; state funds and private loans are the income source.

Note: Information as of 1992.

VIRGINIA

First Nations Development Institute
Navajo/Shiprock Chapter
Lakota Fund, Cherokee Circle Bank
The Stores Building
11917 Main Street
Fredericksburg, VA 22408
(703) 371-5615
(703) 371-5305
Contact: Rebecca Anderson

This organization was founded in 1980 to assist tribes to gain control of their economic future, targeting reservation-based communities nationally. This organization was originally a practitioner, but has since become a referral source.

Technical assistance includes business training courses, individually tailored or selected, peer support and exchange, mentoring, and fund-raising.

Financing is given to individual borrowers. Loan sizes range from $10,000 to $100,000, with an average of $25,000. Loan terms range up to three years. The average term is two years. The interest rate is prime plus 2 percent.

Nonbusiness support services include alcohol abuse/awareness training; training in self-esteem and problem solving; peer support; networking; community organizing; board training; and fund-raising.

Achievements include designing the first microlending fund in the United States. The response from tribes has been great. The individual reservation-based programs have grown dramatically.

First Nations Development Institute plans to increase the number of reservation microlending funds and to expand into housing and land revolving loan funds.

The annual operating budget is $5 to 7 million, and the loan capital fund is $1,000,000.

WASHINGTON

Greater Spokane Business Development Association (GSBDA)
Spokane Area Small Business Loan Program
City Hall, Room 250
Spokane, WA 99201
(509) 625-6325
FAX (509) 625-6315

This organization was founded in 1982, with the small-business loan fund starting in 1991, to encourage and support small business and economic development for Spokane County residents.

Technical assistance includes individual business counseling and providing alternative financing sources.

Financing is given to individual borrowers. Loan sizes range up to $50,000, with an average of $25,000. Loan terms range from one to seven years. The average term is four years.

The Small Business Loan Program acts as an intermediary between the banks and clients by packaging loans, servicing the loans, and administering the program.

Plans are to implement a statewide program, working with the Washington Department of Trade and Economic Development, and to act as a loan-servicing agent for other communities.

The annual operating budget is $200,000, and the loan capital fund is $3.6 million. Sources of funding include 10 area commercial banks, packaging fees, and service charges.

Note: Information as of 1992.

Private Industry Council of Snohomish County
DBA Down Home Washington and Innercity Entrepreneurial Training Program (IETP)
917 134th Street, SW
Everett, WA 98204
(206) 743-9669
Contact: Emily Duncan

This organization was founded in November 1983 to join people and resources to meet employment needs in our communities, targeting residents of timber-dependent communities and low-income minorities in Snohomish County and the central district of Seattle.

Technical assistance includes business training courses, individual business counseling, mentoring, and advisory board internship.

Financing is given to individual borrowers. Loan sizes range up to $5,000, with an average of $3,200. Loan terms range up to five years, with an average of three years.

Nonbusiness support services include child care and transportation.

IETP received a 1988 award for excellence in JTPA programs from the National Associations of Counties.

The operating budget is $200,000. The loan capital fund is $192,000. Sources of funding include foundations, the U.S. Department of Health and Human Services, and state timber funds.

Note: Information as of 1992.

WEST VIRGINIA

Women and Employment
Micro/Small Business Development
601 Delaware Avenue
Charleston, WV 25302
(304) 345-1298
FAX (304) 243-0641
Contact: Pam Curry

This organization was founded in 1980 as a nonprofit, community-based membership organization committed to improving the economic position and quality of life of West Virginia women. Women and Employment works with women in transition, with a special commitment to low-income and minority women. This work is accomplished through direct service action, education and advocacy, or social and economic justice.

Technical assistance includes a business development training course, individual business counseling, peer support and exchange, resource connection, networking, and leadership development.

Women and Employment assisted in 19 business start-ups during the last few years, as well as advocacy, development, and implementation of the state's first Self-Employment Project for AFDC recipients. The West Virginia Women Business Owners Directory also won the 1991 Governor's Partnership for Progress Award for the Hillsboro Community Economic Development Project.

The annual operating budget is $250,000. Funding sources are foundations, governments, contracts, consulting, fund-raising activities, and donations.

Note: Information as of 1992.

WISCONSIN

Cap Services, Inc.
The Self-Employment Project
5499 Highway 10 East
Stevens Point, WI 54481
(715) 345-5208
FAX (715) 345-5206
Contact: John Hay

This agency was founded in 1966 to assist low-income people in attaining economic and emotional self-sufficiency in Marquette, Outagamie, Portage, Waupaca, and Waushare counties.

Technical assistance includes business training courses, individual business counseling, peer support and exchange, business planning, and loan packaging assistance.

Financing is given to individual borrowers. Loan sizes range up to $10,000, with an average of $5,000. Loan terms range up to 10 years, with an average of 3 years.

Nonbusiness support services include child care, transportation, and occupational classroom training.

The project has assisted 13 new businesses that are doing well and are employing a total of 30 people.

CAP Services Self-Employment Project plans to increase the size of its loan fund and obtain increased bank involvement.

The annual operating budget is $3,500,000, and the loan capital fund is $120,000.

Menominee Indian Tribe of Wisconsin
Menominee Revolving Loan Fund
P.O. Box 397
Keshena, WI
(715) 799-5141
FAX (715) 799-4524
Contact: Thomas Litzow

This agency was founded in 1981 to assist Menominee Indians in initiating or expanding projects in the Menominee Reservation that will have a direct economic impact on the tribe and its members.

The fund targets 4,000 tribal members residing on the Menominee Reservation.

Technical assistance includes business training courses, individual business counseling, and mentoring.

Financing is given to individual borrowers. Loan sizes range from $1,000 to $100,000, with and average of $25,000. Loan terms range from 1 to 10 years, with an average term of 5 years.

The annual budget is $50,000. The loan capital fund of $900,000 is funded by Menominee Indian Tribe of Wisconsin and the Bureau of Indian Affairs (BIA).

Newcap, Inc.
Self-Employment Program
1201 Main Street
Oconto, WI
(414) 834-4621
FAX (414) 834-4887
Contact: Kim Rebolledo

This agency was founded in January 1991 and affiliated with the Wisconsin Community Action Association to work toward the elimination of the causes of poverty by enabling and assisting low-income people to attain the skills, motivation, and opportunities necessary for them to become self-sufficient and independent. The target population is 10 counties in Northeast Wisconsin.

Technical assistance includes business training courses, individual business counseling, peer support and exchange, and mentoring.

Nonbusiness support includes individual counseling, child care and transportation.

NEWCAP has operated one business ownership class. Eleven low-income and unemployed individuals completed 128 hours, and all developed and completed a business plan. Several are employed full time, and others are self-employed in their businesses.

NEWCAP will continue the business ownership class, secure new funding for the class, offer the class to more individuals at more locations, and begin to investigate the possibility of operating a loan fund.

The annual operating budget is $3,500,000.

WYOMING

Northern Arapahoe Tribal Credit Program
Credit Committee
P.O. Box 889
Fort Washakie, WY
(307) 332-7744/3059
FAX (307) 332-7543
Contact: Harold Smith

This agency was founded in 1957 to provide services to tribal members who cannot receive services from commercial institutions, targeting enrolled members of the Arapahoe Tribe on the Wind River Indian Reservation.

Technical assistance includes the Emergency Short-Term Loan Program.

Financing which is given to individual borrowers, consists of a loan of $2,000.

The Credit Program has provided this service to the Arapahoe Tribe for almost 40 years.

Plans are to institute a program to provide individuals with loans for livestock, automobiles, and homes.

Note: Information as of 1992.

NATIONAL MICROENTERPRISE PROGRAMS

Association for Enterprise Opportunity (AEO)
353 Folsom Street
San Francisco, CA 94105
(510) 495-6945
FAX (510) 495-7025
Contact: Robert Friedman, chair

AEO was founded on June 22, 1991, to provide its members with a forum and a voice to promote enterprise opportunity for people and communities with limited access to economic resources.

AEO's geographic area is national and includes people and communities with limited access to economic resources.

This agency's achievements include having more than 200 organizational and individual members, and helping spur changes in federal welfare, training, and investment policies.

AEO's future plans include assisting organizations and individuals committed to expanding enterprise opportunity to exchange learning, to influence policy, to communicate, to access funding, and to guide research and evaluation efforts.

The annual budget is $150,000.

Aid to Artisans (ATA)
80 Mountain Spring Road
Farmington, CT 06032
(203) 677-1649
Contact: Clare Brett Smith, president

This organization was founded in 1976 as a nonprofit organization, dedicated to creating employment opportunities for craftspeople in underdeveloped communities around the world.

The target population is craftspeople throughout the world. Services provided by this agency include business training courses in connection with product development production and market research, sales, and long-term sustainability; product development workshops; introduction to the U.S. market; grants to disadvantaged artisan groups; market research; and revival of traditional crafts.

Agency achievements include providing grants to artisan groups in over 30 countries for tools, finance training, and the creation of material banks. ATA completed an economic development project in Honduras that brought more than 200 products to the U.S. market.

ATA identified and trained over 500 artisans, most of whom were rural women, to produce crafts designed from readily available resources. ATA currently has major projects underway all over the world.

The annual operating budget is $700,000.

Center for Community Futures
P.O. Box 5309 Elmwood Station
Berkeley, CA 94705
(510) 540-1928
Contact: James Masters

This agency was founded in October 1981 to assist both nonprofit agencies and individuals to start profit-making businesses.

The geographic area is national and includes public-funded agencies, both non-profit and public.

Business training courses, individual business counseling, peer support and exchange, mentoring, child care, thrift shops, entrepreneurship, and marketing are included in the agency's technical assistance.

The agency's achievements include assisting nonprofits to start and manage their businesses and assisting national associations in capacity building for members. CCF works with agencies in such areas as mental health, employment and training, child care, Head Start, community action agencies, weatherization, area agencies on aging, (PIC/SDAs), United Way, and city and county agencies.

CCF's future plans include providing video tapes, workbooks, and other how-to training materials on such topics as microbusiness loan program creation and operations, marketing, business strategy, and thrift shop and lawn-care businesses.

The annual operating budget ranges from $150,000 to $200,000.

HUB Co-Ventures
(formerly the National Coalition for Women's Enterprise)
101 Alma Street
Apartment 107-8
Palo Alto, CA 94301
(510) 321-7663
FAX (510) 321-7663
Contact: Jing Lyman

This agency was founded in November 1983 to assist communities in building appropriate coalitions and the essential capacity to deliver successful microenterprise programs for those populations locked out of the economic mainstream.

The geographic location is international for women, low-income and physically disadvantaged people, and people of color.

Achievements include promotion of numerous successful direct service programs in the United States, the United Kingdom, and Australia. HUB Co-Ventures now has the basis for an important new database on women's business ownership.

Note: Information as of 1992.

Ms. Foundation for Women
Economic Development Program
141 Fifth Avenue, Sixth Floor
New York, NY 10010
Phone: (212) 353-8580
FAX: (212) 475-4217
Contact: Sara Gould

This organization was begun in 1986 as a national multi-issue, public women's fund, supporting the efforts of women and girls to govern their own lives and influence the world around them. It funds and assists women's self-help organizing efforts and pursues changes in public consciousness, law, philanthropy, and social policy.

The target population is women and other nonprofit organizations assisting low-income women and women of color to become self-sufficient through self-employment and/or employment with others nationally.

Achievements include starting the Economic Development Program; sponsoring an annual national training institute in the field of women and economic development; recently granting $2.2 million to 15 self-employment programs and cooperative businesses; operating a small peer-to-peer internship program; assisting groups on-site with strategic planning and program planning and organizational development issues; and serving as trainer/facilitators at various gatherings of organizations active in the field of self-employment and microenterprise.

The operating budget is as follows: Ms. Foundation for Women, $3 million (including grants) and the Economic Development Program, $500,000 (without grants). Sources of funding include private and corporate foundations, individuals, and limited endowment income.

National Business Incubation Association (NBIA)
One President Street
Athens, OH 45701
(614) 543-4331
FAX (614) 593-1996
Contact: Dinah Adkins

This organization was founded in 1985 to provide training, education, and research for small business incubator developers and managers. It assists the public (including self-employment/microenerprises) in locating the nearest small business incubators.

The target populations include small business incubator developers and managers and those interested in tracking industry or locating small businesses in incubators throughout the United States and Canada.

Achievements include a national conference, regional training, a newsletter, an electronic mail and networking service, information research and referral, publishing, general member services, and a state-of-the-industry survey and report.

NBIA hopes to better serve industry segments ranging from technology incubators for potential high-growth companies to incubators targeted to neighborhood revitalization that assist self-employment/microenterprises.

The annual operating budget of $290,000 is funded by member dues, training reserves, and publication sales.

National Economic Development and Law Center
1950 Addison, #200
Berkeley, CA 94704
(510) 458-2600
FAX (510) 548-7217
Contact: David Kirkpatrick

This agency was founded in 1969 to support a range of community economic development strategies, including microenterprises. It targets low-income individuals throughout the United States.

Technical assistance includes individual business counseling, peer support and exchange, and mentoring.

Achievements include assistance to Women's Initiative for Self-Employment (WISE) and to San Francisco Renaissance, a loan fund serving both programs, and three other programs in development stages.

The annual operating budget is $1.3 million, and the sources of funding include Legal Services Corp. and the Ford Foundation.

Note: Information as of 1992.

National Small Business United
115 15th Street, NW
Suite 710
Washington, DC 20005
(202) 293-87830
FAX (202) 872-8543

This agency was founded in 1937 to advocate the interests of small business before the government. (*Small business* is defined as businesses with 1 to 500 employees.) It is a national lobbying organization with a budget of $1.8 million.

U.S. Department of Labor/Unemployment
Insurance Demonstration Work Group
Unemployment Insurance Self-Employment Demonstration
Washington SEED Project and Massachusetts Enterprise Project
200 Constitution Avenue, NW
Room S-4231
Washington, D.C. 20210
(202) 535-0208
FAX (202) 523-8506
Contact: Jon C. Messenger

This agency was founded in October 1987 to test new and innovative issues of the unemployment insurance (UI) system to assist unemployed workers to return to productive employment. The purpose of the UI Self-Employment Demonstration Project is to determine the viability of self-employment as a reemployment option for unemployed workers, targeting unemployment insurance recipients on permanent layoff. The demonstration sites are in Washington State and Massachusetts.

Technical assistance includes business training in marketing, bookkeeping, finances, individual business counseling, peer support and exchange, entrepreneur club meetings, and business-plan assistance.

Financing grants in Washington State range from $581 to $7,380, with an average of $4,282.

Nonbusiness support services include unlimited individual counseling for the project enrollment period.

UI Demonstration Working Group designed, implemented, and evaluated two self-employment projects and worked on other reemployment demonstration projects. The program is also exploring additional demonstration projects for UI recipients and initiatives to identify and refer UI recipients to reemployment services.

The annual operating budget is $1,000,000, with sources of funding from federal government revenues and state funds.

U.S. Small Business Administration, Office of Women's Business Ownership
409 Third Street, SW
Sixth Floor
Washington, DC 20416
(202) 205-6673
FAX (202) 205-7230

This agency was organized in September 1989 as an umbrella group under the Small Business Administration to establish long-term training and counseling centers to assist small businesses owned by women in their start-up and expansion through technical and financial assistance. Its annual operating budget is $2 million.

Technical assistance includes individual business counseling, peer support and exchange, mentoring, and business training courses.

The demonstration phase of this program is successfully completed, and an extension is anticipated. Plans are to expand the network of long-term training and counseling centers across the country.

Chapter Eight

Developing Community Loan Funds

It's frustrating when you know your business could grow with just a little financial aid and no help is evident. If limited funds are available for entrepreneurs in your geographical area, don't get discouraged. Remember, there are steps you and your peers can take to develop a loan pool in your community. You don't need a finance degree, but you do need volunteers, commitment, and determination.

Approach a new fund as you would any new business; strategic planning is key. Organize a small steering committee; then consider these seven tasks: research existing resources, analyze market needs, investigate options, obtain counseling, organize support/raise money, establish a prototype, and launch a fund.

Research Existing Resources

It's best to avoid duplicating efforts and risking diminishing the local loan capital fund. Nationally, money is available for loan pools. However, those funds are somewhat limited and competition is keen.

Usually, it's not wise to begin a new lending pool where others already exist and are doing a good job. Therefore, it is important to thoroughly research what *is* available in your community before starting a new venture.

Organize a small group of interested individuals. Perhaps your local chamber of commerce will assist by sponsoring a steering committee. Brainstorm all possible current funding resources. As a suggestion, you might want to call area small business bankers, credit unions, industrial banks, state economic offices, local Small Business Development Centers, and the SBA. National offices listed in Chapter Seven, such as the Association for Enterprise Opportunity, can give you information on any area microenterprise loan funds.

As you gather existing finance information, develop a written schedule that shows the funding type, who qualifies for a loan, loan limits, collateral required, terms, technical assistance offered, and any other specific criteria. Be sure to include the total capital pool for each organization, the number and amount of loans outstanding, the average loan size and term, as well as how much money is available to lend this fiscal year.

Analyze the Market

If you have enough volunteers, a second group can develop a community small business borrowers' survey simultaneously with the group researching resources. Include necessary vital statistics for local small firms, such as annual business dollar volume, the number of employees and the current business status (i.e., start-up, part-time, emerging, home-based, etc.). Consider asking these questions too:

- What are your typical borrowing needs? Term?
- Have you applied for a bank loan in the last year? Amount? Results?
- If you were denied a loan, what were the reasons given?
- Did you seek funding from any other sources? Who? Amount? Results?
- Can you provide business collateral for a loan and adequate cash flow for loan repayment?
- Can you provide personal collateral for a business loan?
- Does your business need assistance in other areas, such as business plan development, accounting, marketing? If yes, list the items in order of importance.
- Do you think your neighborhood location impacts your ability to get financing? Is there a bank in your neighborhood?
- Have you taken any business classes in the last year? Are you willing to attend classes as part of a loan program?
- Are you willing to counsel others in your field of expertise?
- If a new community loan pool is created, will you support it? Volunteer your time? Consider moving your business bank account?

There may be other issues relevant to your particular area. For example:

- Business owner ethnicity/sex. Keep in mind that certain funds are available for women/minority-owned businesses as well as socially or economically disadvantaged businesses in some situations.
- Dominant industry. It could be important if your community is dependent on one business type. Industry-specific economies such as agriculture, technology, and artisans have different funding needs and resources.

When developing the questionnaire, get opinions from experts. Local colleges or extension services might offer good advice and/or provide students to assist your efforts. Bankers, CPAs, lawyers, and social workers could all voice interesting viewpoints.

Remember, too, that other communities have gone through this process. Don't "reinvent the wheel" if it's not necessary. The SBA, state development offices, and many national associations can give you solid leads on survey resources.[1]

Investigate Options

As you design your fund prototype, keep an open mind. Don't limit your choices. Look at every possible alternative; then select one or two that would best serve your community. Workable loan funds vary greatly.

The following examples should give you some ideas and get you off to a good start:

Family circles. This is a very old process used worldwide by many cultures. It is informal by nature and requires as few as five to seven borrower participants.

---

[1]Try: Association for Enterprise Opportunity, National Chamber of Commerce, National Federation of Community Development Credit Unions, Federal Reserve Bank, National Homebased Business Association, National Association of Independent Businesses as well as trade-specific associations. Further information regarding resources used as examples in this chapter are found in the chapter addendum.

Basically, a group forms around the notion that they will depend on one another for small loans. A meeting time is arranged; generally, it's once a week. At that meeting, each member contributes a set amount of money. One individual at a time is designated to use those proceeds. He or she must repay the loan pool in full, with interest, by an agreed-upon date. Weekly installments are usually required. No collateral is pledged; however, peer pressure is tremendous. A member may not miss a meeting or a loan payment.

As time goes on, the loan pool grows substantially. The group may opt to formalize loan paperwork, open a bank account, and give technical assistance to members. At some point, the assembly may spin off and form subgroups, with original members as new circle leaders.

Another variation of this technique is known as peer group lending. In some models, an individual begins the fund with a small amount of capital. As the "bank", that person lends money to borrowers in need of funds and without resources. When the borrower repays the loan, he, or more often she, joins "the bank" as a stockholder in the fund.

One famous example of this group lending formula is the Grameen Bank of Bangladesh. Its founder, Muhammed Yu-nus, won a 1994 Nobel Prize for building the economy of a nation "one dollar at a time." To date, more than one million participants received loans from the Grameen Bank.

Other examples of this process include: Accion "Solidarity Circles" in Latin America; and "N-jangi" groups in Cameroon, Africa. Much more structured U.S. variations of peer group funding include: Accion, Bedford-Styverson, New York; Women's Circle Project, Los Angeles, California; and MiCasa, Denver, Colorado. (See Chapter Seven, "Microenterprise Lending Programs.")

Barter/exchange town currency.   "Dollars" aren't always the answer. Some communities have a talented work force but still suffer from high unemployment. When that happens, local families have time on their hands and limited dollars to spend. Local merchants have goods and services but few customers.

One small town in upstate New York helped curb that situation. Founded by local resident Paul Glover, "Ithaca Money" is based on principles established in Depression-era America that allowed communities to legally print their own currency to exchange for goods and services.

A few years ago, this revitalization program gave an economically depressed community a jump-start. In Ithaca, New York, plumbers, for example, could collect all or part of their fees in "Ithaca Money." That payment then could be used as "cash" at any participating local merchant. Purchases could include dinner at a favorite restaurant or kids' school shoes. Today, at least a dozen communities throughout the United States use the Ithaca model. One such program in Boulder, Colorado, uses "Boulder Hours" to effectively increase the minimum wage for all participants to $10 per hour.

Founder Jhym Phoenix assigned a one-tenth hour time value to each "dollar." Therefore a $10 "Boulder Hour" bill is exchangeable for $10 retail goods or one hour of service.

Keep in mind, community barter/exchanges can be established as citywide nonprofits or formal, for-profit business networks. Some groups charge membership fees while others collect a percentage on items exchanged. (See Chapter Three, "Alternative Nonbank Financing Options.")

Community credit unions. Credit Unions are nonprofit associations owned and operated by members. Technically, a common bond must exist among members. For example, many locations have a state teachers credit union.

Small businesses may join together to form a credit union. Communities may have an association within established geographical boundaries.

In some ways, credit unions operate much like commercial banks. They provide checking and savings accounts as well as make loans. They differ from banks in that they are nonprofits owned by members. Owners serve on various committees and oversee all fund activities.

Credit unions may be state or federally chartered. Getting one off the ground requires a group of volunteers who act as organizers for the first year or two. Credit union deposits can be insured by the Federal Credit Union Share Insurance Fund.

Co-operatives.   Artisan guilds are good examples of this joint venture procedure. Many artists share marketing expenses, such as advertising, invitations, refreshments, and space rental for arts and crafts shows. Some exhibit together year-round.

Most groups function as cooperatives. A formal organization with a board of directors, written rules, and designated responsibilities seems to work best.

One such organization, the Waterford Artisans, became so successful at co-op development that it began bidding on contracts with major department stores and state governments for items such as hand-made quilts and miniature state flags. Thriving in its rural community, the group solicits and adds temporary employees when large orders need filling.

This concept works well when the goal is community cooperation. Solid organization is key to success.

Capital funds.   Capital funds are an extension of traditional commercial lending availability in any community. Generally, these funds provide loan pools for a market segment whose needs are not being met by local commercial lenders.

There are several approaches to capital funds. Two examples follow:

Partnerships with banks.   As discussed in Chapter Two, banks are often caught between regulation and a desire to serve their communities. Capital fund partnerships provide one good solution for this dilemma.

With a community nonprofit taking the lead, local banks can participate by pledging a set number of dollars each to a community fund. These pledges are generally credit lines made available to the nonprofit for a reasonable term and at a discount interest rate.

The fund is managed by the nonprofit; bank representatives serve on the advisory board. Several successful partnerships exist in the United States. Two good examples are the Denver Partnership Capital Fund in Denver, Colorado, and Working Capital in Manchester, New Hampshire.

Private corporations. A private corporation may also organize to serve community lending needs. One such group, Colorado Capital Initiative, Inc. (CCI), is a nonprofit formed to "help economically underdeveloped communities by providing small businesses with access to credit and business assistance."

This corporation works independently as a consulting, training, and lending group. CCI has private stockholders who accept risks and participate in profits. CCI encourages local commercial banks to make small business loans by providing those banks with private loan guarantees from its stockholders and additional guarantors. This program also enhances the lender's "comfort level" by giving the borrowers technical assistance over the life of the loan.

CCI leverages local loan funds at a 12:1 ratio by spreading the risks through outside secondary market shares.

Community development block grants. CDBGs make funds available to companies that meet criteria established by the U.S. Department of Housing and Urban Development (HUD). Essentially, those requirements are to provide jobs and build the economy in an area that is at least 51 percent low to moderate income. Individual business grants may be as much as $250,000.

Communities may also participate in the Community Development Block Grant program. Many of these projects are managed through state government loan funds. You can obtain information through HUD or your state.

The foregoing examples are listed to pique your interest. However, they are just the beginning. Review Chapter Seven, "Microenterprise Lending Programs." Don't limit your reading to just your home state. Many interesting, diverse programs exist throughout the country. A quick look at those programs will give you ideas, names, and phone numbers.

Obtain Counseling

After you review several programs, narrow your options. Select one or two approaches for follow-up.

Before you proceed, make sure you have your survey results tabulated, so that you know what is available in your community and what local small business owners need. Look for program gaps, and avoid duplication.

When you have a thorough understanding of your options and requirements, it's time to call in experts. Remember, other communities have gone through this process. Their experiences can save you time, energy, and money.

Hopefully, you garnered contacts and good information while investigating fund ideas. Go back to those individuals and ask for recommendations. Many groups will give you free advice, and some will provide you with complete written materials so that you may duplicate their program. Both are invaluable services that benefit your community.

A few organizations make extra money for their own projects by consulting with new groups. Still others will give you names of individual freelance professionals who helped them.

Depending on your goals and finances, there are a couple different approaches.

- If your volunteer group has time to complete legwork, you might contract a minimum number of hours with an expert. That individual could help lay out a strategy for your project. A steering committee could perform the tasks.

- If you have more cash resources than time, you could hire a consulting group to review your findings and design a complete program.

These are some things a program consultant can do for your community lending fund:

- Provide an overview and documentation for several existing programs. Explain strengths and weaknesses of each one.

- Evaluate your community surveys and compare them to other project data. Help design a solid program based on your needs.

- Plan a realistic time table to get your program up and running.

- Help you identify likely funding sources within your community.

- Recommend foundations that work with other microenterprise lending funds that might work with you.

Raise Money

While it's never easy to raise money, community loan funds might have more local appeal than you expect. There are several advantages:

- Community funds are not charities; they help create jobs.
- A fund improves the local economy.
- Bank participation helps fulfill the commercial Community Reinvestment Act requirement.
- Big companies can help small companies at arm's length.
- A revolving loan-type program keeps putting money back into the community for future lending.
- Several major foundations currently participate in micro-enterprise programs. The Small Business Administration sponsors a microloan demonstration project, too.

Use good judgment when you plan your fund-raising campaign. Get advice from existing lending programs; then thoroughly plan your approach and time table.

It helps to follow a few basic money raising rules:

- Make an appointment with a potential contributor; don't "drop in."
- Rehearse a three to five minute presentation.
- Leave a short written proposal that reiterates key points.
- Follow up with a phone call in a week or less.
- Whether or not you are successful with a contact, ask that person for the names of at least three others he or she would recommend as potential fund contributors/investors.
- Prepare short public service announcements (PSAs) for your local radio and television stations to help spread the word.

Establish a Prototype

This is one of the most important steps for any community fund. It's likely everyone on your steering committee will be anxious to put plans into action. Remember, however, that caution is the by-word. Go slowly. Test your program carefully, and get expert advice and reviews.

Launch Your Fund

When you are ready, open the doors! Keep in mind that other funds can learn from your experiences. Maintain good records, consider a simple computer-generated monthly or bi-monthly newsletter, and build a mailing list of potential clients and investors.

Write short, informative articles for the local newspapers about your work. Announce the names of your technical assistance graduates. At least once a year, hold an open house for dignitaries, highlighting fund participants' accomplishments.

Remember, too, that your group will benefit from membership in national organizations. Those groups lobby Congress, teach classes, conduct practioner forums, publish membership rosters, and continuously provide your lending fund with up-to-date microenterprise data.

As your loan pool grows successfully, consider these three important steps:

1. Sell your loan portfolios on a secondary market so that funds are continuously returned to your community.[2]

2. Spin off your program in nearby locales. Get neighboring municipalities involved.

3. Teach, consult with, and help outside groups to develop their programs.

If it seems like an insurmountable task, take heart from 29-year-old Fordham University law student, Matthew Lee. According to recent reports, Lee single-handedly contracted *$50 million in loan commitments for poor residents of the South Bronx.*[3]

---

[2]One organization that buys nonprofit loans is the Community Reinvestment Fund. Based in Minneapolis, Minnesota, CRF purchases loan portfolios and packages and sells them in large blocks. It's a good idea to contact CRF when designing your lending fund. That way you can be sure your program meets appropriate criteria from the outset.

[3]Associated Press, *Denver Post*, Monday, November 14, 1994, p. 3A.

He accomplished this remarkable task by simply using the banks' own loan records to show a history of neighborhood neglect, a practice that is not tolerated under the present Community Reinvestment Act rules. Tackling some of New York City's largest banks, Lee is an inspiration.

Community funds are born of grassroots needs and desires. Your ideas and contributions are important because they have a powerful ripple effect. Your hard work will pay off in more small businesses, new jobs, and an enriched local economy.

The ball's in your court. You *can* do it! Go for it. All it takes is a little courage, an independent spirit, and entrepreneurial determination. Do it now.

"Somebody said that it couldn't be done,

But he with a chuckle replied

That 'maybe it couldn't,' but he would be one

Who wouldn't say so till he tried.

So he buckled right in with the trace of a grin

On his face. If he worried, he hid it.

He started to sigh as he tackled the thing

That couldn't be done,

And he did it."

— Edgar A. Guest

CHAPTER EIGHT RESOURCES

Accion International
130 Prospect Street
Cambridge, MA
(617) 492-4930

American Association of Home-Based Businesses
P.O. Box 10023
Rockville, MD 20849
(800) 447-9710
(202) 310-3130

Coalition for Women's Economic Development (CWED)
Solidarity Circle
315 West Ninth Street, Suite 705
Los Angeles, CA 90015
(213) 489-4995

Colorado Capital Initiatives, Inc.
330 Seventeenth Street, Suite 5300
Denver, CO 80202
(303) 628-3800

Community Reinvestment Fund
2400 Foshay Tower
821 Marquett Avenue
Minneapolis, MN 55402
(612) 338-3050

Downtown Denver Partnership, Inc. Capital Fund
511 16th Street
Denver, CO 80202
(303) 534-6161

Federal Reserve Bank Board of Governors
20th Constitution Avenue
Washington, DC 20551
(202) 452-3000

Mi Casa Resource Center for Women
The Business Center for Women
571 Galapago Street
Denver, CO 80204
(303) 595-0422

National Association of Enterprise Opportunity
353 Folsom Street
San Francisco, CA 94105
(510) 495-6945

National Federation of Community Development Credit Unions (NFCDCU)
120 Wall Street, Tenth Floor
New York, NY 10005
(212) 809-1850

National Federation of Independent Business
600 Maryland SW, Suite 700
Washington, DC 20024
(202) 554-9000

Santa Cruz Community Credit Union (SCCCU)
512 Front Street
Santa Cruz, CA 95060
(408) 425-7708

Shorebank Advisory Services
1950 East 71st Street
Chicago, IL 60649
(312) 288-0066

U.S. Chamber of Commerce
1615 H Street NW
Washington, DC 20062
(202) 659-6000

Working Capital
2500 North River Road
Manchester, NH 03106
(603) 644-3124

RESOURCES

For additional information about factoring, contact:

National Commercial Finance Association
225 West 34th Street, Suite 1815
New York, NY 10122
(212) 594-3490

For additional information about bartering, contact:

International Reciprocal Trade Assocation (IRTA)
6305 Hawaii Court
Alexandria, VA 22312
(703) 237-1802

ITEX Exchange
P.O. Box 2309
Portland, OR 97208
(800) 225-ITEX

For additional information about venture capital, contact:

National Association of Small Business Investment Companies
1199 North Fairfax Street
Alexandria, VA 22314
(703) 683-1601

National Association of Investment Companies
1111 14th Street NW, Suite 700
Washington, DC 20005
(202) 289-4336

For additional information about public offerings, contact:

Office of Public Affairs
U.S. Securities and Exchange Commission
Washington, DC 20549
(202) 942-0020

For additional information about franchising, contact:

International Franchise Association
1350 New York Avenue NW, Suite 900
Washington, DC 20005
(202) 628-8000
For a free catalogue listing various publications for sale: (800) 543-1038

For additional information about foreign investments, contact:

Exporting Counseling
U.S. Department of Commerce
Washington, DC 20549
(202) 482-4811

World Trade Centers Association
One World Trade Center
New York, NY 10048
(212) 755-1370

Index

Other books of interest to you from Irwin Professional Publishing...

THE BUSINESS OWNER'S GUIDE TO ACHIEVING FINANCIAL SUCCESS

David A. Duryee

Addressing the four "phases" of a business—start-up, high growth, maturity, and renewal—this book shows owners how to analyze their financial condition and statement of cash flow, plan and manage for growth, anticipate seasonal cash flow needs, and effectively plan for investments in fixed assets.
ISBN: 0-7863-0228-3

THE BUSINESS OWNER'S GUIDE TO ACHIEVING FINANCIAL SUCCESS WORKBOOK

David A. Duryee

This workbook is designed to accompany the textbook and contains a complete set of forms that take you step-by-step through the historical analysis and the short- and long-range planning process.
ISBN: 0-7863-0338-7

SMALL BUSINESS SUCCESS THROUGH TQM

Terry Ehresman

Offers a practical, easy-to-follow approach to training the workforce of any small business in the tools and concepts of TQM.
ISBN: 0-87389-309-3

RAISING CAPITAL
Grant Thornton's Guide for Entrepreneurs

Michael C. Bernstein and Lester Wolosoff

This book describes the financing options available to companies along with many of the issues that must be addressed when considering sources such as banks, angels, venture capital firms, and government agencies as well as providing guidance about preparing business plans and information concerning accounting issues that can arise in connection with public offerings.
ISBN: 0-7863-0150-3

Available in fine bookstores and libraries everywhere.